ENDORS

Weaving together scripture with his own personal stories of success and failure, Keith renews our minds on the topic of spiritual warfare and trains us to battle with mighty new covenant weapons like praise, joy, love, and wisdom. The concepts presented in this book are as revolutionary to the subject of spiritual warfare as John Paul Jackson's *Needless Casualties of War,* and Graham Cooke's *Way of the Warrior* series. Thank you, Keith, for helping us fight the good fight of faith in a healthy and powerful way.

DAN McCOLLAM
Prophetic trainer, author, and founder of Sounds of the Nations and the Prophetic Company.

The great theologian C.S. Lewis once said regarding the devil, "There are two equal and opposite errors into which our race can fall about the devils. One is to disbelieve in their existence. The other is to believe and have an excessive and unhealthy interest in them." Our ability as believers to have a healthy perspective and victorious mindset in regard to spiritual warfare is absolutely vital to everyone who desire to live a victorious life. Keith Ferrante has written a blueprint that will launch you into a victorious life of advancing the Kingdom of heaven against unseen realities. This book is both practical, yet full of deep spiritual truths that will equip and activate you to become the spiritual warrior you were created to be!

MATT GONZALES
President and Co-founder of Kingdom Culture Ministries

Keith usually asks me to endorse his books and I am always thrilled to read and comment on his books. Each one seems better and more relevant than the last and I always think he continually knocks it out of the ball park!!!! Keith is a spiritual son who is writing what I wish I could and I am proud of how he continually is clarifying and mentoring prophetic ministry. Growing up as a southern baptist who was taught and loved word, I had no mentoring when the prophetic call and ministry was released in my heart and spirit. That's why I value and honor Keith for what he is doing in the kingdom. I made many mistakes not having any mentors. This book is one of Keith's best, with theological foundations along with testimonies and stories. This is a must read and will really help the reader grow and mature in the prophetic!!! Well done son and I am proud to call you son!!!!!

WENDELL McGOWAN
Prophetic Ministry, Prophetic Company School

I've known Keith as a friend for a few years now and have watched how he engages the heavenly realm and deals with spiritual conflict. This book is a true reflection of how he operates. In his book Overcoming Keith offers a refreshingly unique, joy-filled perspective on the matter of spiritual warfare. Much has been written on this topic and yet Keith brings a much-needed new covenant approach that will equip and empower you to effectively engage the spirit realm.

PEDRO ADAO
Founder of the 100X Academy: The #1 Training Program and Community for Kingdom Entrepreneurs

Published by *Emerging Prophets*
Contact *admin@emergingprophets.com, EmergingProphets.com*
Cover design *Sam Arts*
Editing *Krista Dunk*
Interior Layout *Olivier Darbonville*

Printed in the United States of America

OVER COMING

A VICTORIOUS APPROACH —— TO —— SPIRITUAL WARFARE

KEITH FERRANTE

CONTENTS

INTRODUCTION

My Name is Keith. The name Keith means Meant for Battle! I've always been a fighter. It doesn't matter what I do, I'm not going to quit until I win. It doesn't mean I always win, but God gave me a fighting spirit. I have learned that I have the gift of breaking through the enemy's camp and taking territory. This is a God-given spirit that I want to impart to you in this book.

There are too many folks getting beat up as believers, and they don't know anything about war. We are in a war. Whether we want to believe it or not, the New Covenant era that we entered into through the victory he won on the cross did not end battle for us. If that were so, why would Paul talk so much about warfare? In Ephesians 6:12 Paul says, "For our struggle is not against flesh and blood…" So, we know that we are in a fight. But it is how we fight that determines our victory. We must learn to fight from victory and with the right weapons that will ensure us victory in a New Covenant way.

First of all, too many people get clobbered because they don't believe they are in a fight. Secondly, some people get defeated because they are using the wrong weapons. Thirdly, some people are getting defeated because they don't know what the real battle is. There is a deception out there that says we don't need to fight. That deception says that we have received the grace of God, and therefore have entered into a finished work that doesn't need anything else but wonderfully blissful fun. I like wonderful, blissful fun and will talk about the power of fun later on, but Scripture says in 1 Peter 5:8-9 that the enemy prowls around like a roaring lion looking for whom he may devour. This passage also says resist him. There are many scriptures with this message, leading me to believe that we have to be strong, alert, on guard and attentive. This is serious business.

We are in a battle, friends. It's a good fight, but it is a fight. We are called to take territory. I don't know if you have been watching the world around you, but do you notice that the young generation is being deceived by immoral media? Do you see that the enemy rages to turn us against one another? Do you see the enemy is fighting in this generation to breed division, suspicion, murder and hate? He has created laws that sanction murder of innocent babies, changing of humanity's identity and legislation legalizing drugs that destroy people's lives under the deception of helping them. Some argue that political laws should be created to protect the rights of every person no matter how immoral they are. Yes, some laws should be created to protect the dignity of humankind. But the Word of God always has to be the guiding force of even the world's systems, otherwise demonic portals are opened when laws are legislated that validate sin. Like a biological parent, government has the authority of a parent when they make laws. When they validate something, the children of the sphere they govern can have a portal opened up over them connected to whatever spirit is behind the laws they are validating.

I'll say it like this. Years ago, I went to another country for several months and felt such purity in my mind and thoughts. When I flew back into my home state of California, I immediately was hit with lust and shame. I didn't realize, until those thoughts were absent from the battle over my mind, that they weren't my thoughts. They were the thoughts of the state I lived within: California. That may be provoking to some and even disbelief could hit you right now over that concept. "How could that be fair?" you may ask. It isn't, because the devil never fights fair.

That is why war is at hand, folks. You can either hide in caves, sometimes caves are church buildings, or awaken to your God-given task of taking the territory around you that the enemy currently rules. When I youth pastored, my eyes were opened and my heart sobered over the devastating bondage many of our charismatic, prophetic, worship-loving youth were under. I saw them sexting, (which I didn't even know existed). Maybe I was ignorant, or maybe I was set apart. Actually, I was set apart, like a Nazarite.

I remember one of my mentors, Kris Vallotton, saying years ago that very thing. "Who set you apart, Keith? Somebody did." Yes, I was set apart by my parents and grandparents to the Lord. I have always been his. I have always had a passion for purity, holiness and pleasing God. It took me some years to realize that holiness and purity were given as a gift that then needed to be protected.

So, when I got into the youth group and saw the moral decay that had actually been given to them (through ungodly youth leaders who had prophecy, worship, etc., but were not completely honest and set apart) I was devastated. Injustice rose up in me. Not only were they bound down by sexting, immorality and all sorts of identity confusion, but they were also smoking pot and injecting other drugs and alcohol into their systems. My heart cried out over this injustice. I thought, "Don't their parents know about this?" Some of the parents were Holy Ghost-filled believers. But I realized our youth were getting taken because we hadn't won the battle we were called to win.

As I jumped into the trenches of trying to restore the purity of the kids I was entrusted with, I realized I couldn't just fight the battle of the youth group. I realized I'd have to go to the high places. The government was the one that first stood out to me as important. It seemed so daunting, so unattainable. How could little old me do anything about the government? But that has been a part of my journey.

I have since been to numerous government functions – sometimes just coming to support a believing senator and other times prophesying over numbers of government workers and leaders. I don't fully know how we are going to get back the systems of this world that we seem to be so outnumbered in. But my heart now knows that the battle I am called to is not just for me and my family. The battle is for generations of people who currently live and will live after me.

Folks, we are called to engage in the battle of our generation. We can't just blindly hide, thinking like Hezekiah did that, "Oh good, I'm glad that there will be peace in my lifetime. The next generation will take care of itself, so I'll just live for today." Isaiah 39:8 recounts this:

"'The word of the Lord you have spoken is good,' Hezekiah replied.
For he thought, 'There will be peace and security in my lifetime.'"

No! We have to choose to engage the war that is upon us. There is war all around. There is war for your family, war over your destiny, war for your most precious relationships, war over your finances, war over your city, war over your nation, and there is war over nations and the generations to come. I've spent many years fighting battles against the impurity and poverty that came through my family line. I fought those demons because I wanted my children and the generations that I affect to have my life's victories as a covering and protection for them. I didn't want my children and those after me to have to fight those battles just because I decided they were too painful to fight. No, I knew that if I didn't fight those battles, then they would be tormented with the same demons that tormented me. Fathers fight battles. Are you a father? Mothers fight battles for their children. Are you one of those fighter moms? We need you to be. We need warriors.

I've learned to fight and have the battle scars to prove it. I want you to read in this book about the battles I've fought well and the battles I didn't fight well, the victories I've won and the battles I've lost. I want you to learn from my journey so you can learn to fight in a New Covenant way. I want you to be provoked to realize that you have to fight. I want you to be provoked to awaken out of hiding. For those not hiding, I want you who are already fighting to have greater tools for higher effectiveness.

I know I don't have all the keys for successful warfare, but I know I have some. May you be infused with the New Covenant warfare spirit that Jesus gave us when he said in Matthew 28:19, "Go and make disciples of nations." That mandate was a declaration of war. The nations all around us have been ruled by the enemy for too long. It's our job to make the kingdoms and nations of this world God's. I pray that you would be infused with boldness and courage to join me on this journey in recapturing the territory that belongs to the Lord. I'll start our journey by sharing about a life-changing, or should I say eye-opening, 400-mile prayer walk I had the privilege to be a part of.

May his Kingdom come to earth!

Keith Ferrante

CHAPTER ONE

ANOTHER METHOD
OF WARFARE

About 15 years ago, there was a prayer walk I participated in led by one of my mentors. It was more than a leisurely stroll, spanning all the way from the Oregon border to San Francisco, California. What a privilege it was for me to join them after the first week and walk with them several hundred miles all the way to San Francisco.

The team of seven who had come over from the UK were seasoned prophetic intercessors. They had come over to walk 30 miles a day for three weeks, in a territory they didn't even live in, and pray. That blew me away. Being a zealous young man, I joined them for a weeks-worth of walking. I quickly realized that 30 miles a day is an incredible amount of walking.

The first day I joined in with a very competitive spirit, deciding I was going to be the fastest walker and beat one of the UK team members who was around my age. Not very grand motives for why I was walking…ha ha… although I also had other reasons that were more "spiritual." Interestingly enough, the first day I injured my foot. For two weeks I had to nurse the foot along and carried an injury in that foot for about a year afterwards.

What I learned in that situation was that competitiveness and jealousy can be closely aligned and in the wrong settings can open a door for the enemy to injure your feet. I experienced it here as well as have seen it in other situations with other people. Wrong spiritual attitudes in the midst of taking spiritual territory can affect your body.

STRUCK DOWN BUT NOT DESTROYED

Nevertheless, the foot injury didn't stop me from being a part of this monumental time. God had me there for a reason. There were lots of valid, verified signs and wonders that followed the prayer walk. One sign was an area of land that had been taken from the First Nations people. This land was returned back to them the day after that area had been walked through. There were other amazing, miraculous signs. One city we stopped at, Sonoma, we were praying and repenting for sins committed by the English, the Spanish and the First Nations people. When that prayer time was going on, I looked across the park where we were praying, and the Lord highlighted a random person. As I gazed at this man who was walking by on crutches, God said he would heal him as a sign of what our prayers had accomplished that day.

I went over to the man and asked him what was wrong with him. "Why are you on crutches?" He shared that he walked with crutches because he had polio. I prayed for him and he was healed. He physically changed and didn't need his crutches after the prayer was done. Afterwards as we talked, the conversation turned towards his nationality. He shared that he had English, Spanish and First Nations DNA in him. Those were the same three people groups we had just been praying and repenting over. What a testimony. God had indeed healed this man as a sign that he had healed the land as well!

Along with these great testimonies, there was warfare. I was new to seeing things in the spirit, and one day as we passed a Buddhist retreat center, I saw a dragon coming at me in the spirit. The method of dealing with strongholds we used during many of those encounters was the casting down method. We would bind and cast down the stronghold spirits over those areas. I remember being so provoked as we walked into and then past that ornate, gold-trimmed shrine. As our prayer warrior team walked, each day I had a plastic bottle of water I carried. In that dragon-sensing moment, I violently threw my water bottle onto the ground, it splintered and the water burst out. It's hard for a plastic water bottle to break like that, but it shows how provoked in my spirit I was to deal with the spirits over the area.

Weeks later, a random person who knew nothing about that situation, saw in the Spirit that when I threw a bottle to the ground, the anointing increased in my life. That was quite a confirmation.

There were other moving events along the way. I remember one hill named after a snake. While walking on the hill, one of the prophets forcefully cast down the spirit over that area. During those times of seeing this group exercise powerful spiritual authority, I was energized and felt invincible. I'm so thankful for the warriors from the UK who fought alongside us for our land.

The walk finally came to an end with me having the privilege of leading the larger group of 40 across the Golden Gate Bridge and finishing at the Catholic Mission in the center of town. After we crossed the bridge, we were joined by one of Lou Engle's intercessors who had been a part of a group walking from the California/Mexico border all the way up to San Francisco, retracing the Spanish Missions. He was a fierce intercessor, and he told me as I led that it was time to get focused in order for us to finish strong, because this was battle.

WHAT A MOMENT

On our last stretch, we walked at high-velocity speeds, praying loudly and intensely for California to be restored. We passed a lady sitting on a bench and she shouted at us, "Shut up!" Without missing a step, he quickly countered her demonically-inspired remarks with, "If we are silent, the rocks will cry out!"

How cool was that experience – to be able to be a part of history! Our three-week walk ended that day, and I went back to my pastoral post and my dear UK friends went back home.

Within a week of going home, more warfare came. One of the warriors on the trip found out they had contracted cancer…nine months later, dying on Valentine's Day. It was devastating news, but it's like their death was a seed sown in the ground for the harvest of California. I also battled internal backlash for a whole month after getting home, feeling slaughtered while stationed at my little outpost town of Willits, CA.

One day, when battling the spiritual forces retaliating against me from the prayer walk, the Lord quietly told me, "I didn't tell you to battle that way." I instantly knew what way he meant: the method of casting down principalities, etc. He then went on and told me, "Don't you remember what I have been teaching you? I've been teaching you to battle with praise." There was no judgement or even theology against the method of casting down principalities. However, he reminded me that he had another method for *me*.

You see, I had been in training by the Lord for months to battle another way. He had been teaching me to battle with praise. My 11 years in Willits was a season of learning to battle with wisdom and with the right weapons. At the end of our 11 years in Willits, the Lord told me something unique. He said, "Keith, I want you to go back to before the battle started." I said,

"When was that Lord?" He said, "When you started going after worship." Wow! What a revelation, and what a sobering way to learn the lesson. He had been teaching me the power of praise and worship to gain victory. On a prayer walk for California, I witnessed an effective warfare method, but I was learning through the backlash I faced afterwards that maybe there was another way: the way of praise.

Now, don't get me wrong. There was genuine fruit on that walk. Without a doubt that walk gave me an authority in California. I know the signs and wonders we experienced in that walk were valid. Binding and casting down warfare got results. I know that walk achieved many things in the spirit... and yet I know the Lord was showing me there was another way, a different way for me. This way is where I would be more protected, more covered and have less retaliation and backlash coming at me. I was a warrior, but I needed to learn the weapons of the New Covenant Warrior.

THE WEAPON OF PRAISE

During that season, the Lord taught me many things about the power of praise. I had been going through a whole month of warfare. "What does that warfare look like," you might ask? For me in that situation, it looked like thoughts of impurity and fear clobbering me daily, hourly, and often. Those thoughts intensely warred against me, and I felt at every moment that I was on the defensive. I couldn't even go to the mall or out in public for fear I would be assaulted with lust or taken out by intimidation from the devil; intimidation over protection concerning my family's safety. Intimidation was trying to make me feel like the devil was so big and powerful, but I was powerless.

For several years I had been warring to get victory over strongholds that had been in my family line and my personal history; strongholds of fear and impurity. It was important to me to be a Joseph. Joseph walked free of the strongholds of his family line, and then established a breakthrough for his family: the nations and the generations to come. But the enemy was internally clobbering me, relentlessly.

In the moment when I felt I could handle no more, I heard the Lord. He spoke to me as I was in my car on the way home to Willits. I had stopped in Santa Rosa and was hungry. I wanted to stop and eat at the mall, but was afraid to go inside; afraid I wouldn't be able to handle my battle. Sometimes the thoughts during warfare seem so silly, so immature. But during those battles, they are very real and can determine your future based on how you win or lose those mind wars. Thankfully the Lord knows how much we can handle. He spoke to me when I was maxed out in my attempt to be victorious over those thoughts. He gave me one simple thought, one simple verse: "Psalm 18:3." That was it. I didn't even know the verse. I quickly found my Bible, opened up the passage and read it.

Fresh hope rose up within me. There before me was the very weapon needed for that battle. "I called to the Lord, who is worthy of praise, and I have been saved from my enemies."

In an instant I knew what to do. In my car in the mall parking lot, I screamed out, "Jesus!" It didn't matter who was around me. I was desperate for victory. I shouted praises in that car, lifting up my hands and releasing the desperate cry of praise to a good Father – the only one who could rescue me. When I released my praise in that parking lot, heaven ran to my aid. I felt the warfare instantly lift and a holy boldness fell upon me. I was free; I could tell. The tormenting thoughts were gone! Wow! Jesus! You are amazing!

BOLDNESS RETURNED

Immediately boldness returned and it was time to make the enemy pay. I got out of my car and went into the restaurant, knowing I was pure and

I was powerful. I ordered my food, while telling the people around me about Jesus. The devil was going to pay for that month-long battle. I wanted recompense for all the mental pain he had caused me.

Do you know what Scripture calls this kind of mental pain? Suffering. Several times in the book of Peter, suffering in the Greek is defined as *mental vexation*. There is a suffering that goes on when the enemy attacks you. Scripture says that when you suffer, you should expect to be rewarded. Having the enemy target your mind isn't fun, but it is necessary for your spiritual muscles to grow in how to resist him.

Sometimes when we suffer in this kind of warfare, it is self-inflicted (because we chose a path that wasn't the best for us – even in my case when I was doing spiritual warfare in an unauthorized way), and sometimes we are doing everything right and still get assaulted. Either way, it is important to learn the right weapons to use. I had been learning that in certain battles I needed to praise.

Paul and Silas are great examples of this kind of praise. In Acts 16, the two men were in an interesting situation. They had just confronted a woman who had been hounding them for days, repeatedly declaring they were men of God for all to hear. She was declaring facts, but from a lying spirit. That gets irritating and they were fed up. When Paul could handle it no longer, he rebuked the spirit in her and it came out. That spirit had been giving the owners of that lady a lot of money, and now they were mad at Paul. They threw Paul and Silas into prison. But at midnight, in chains, they were singing praises. All of a sudden, God showed up and an earthquake shook the prison doors open. They got free and the prison guard and others got saved. Wow, the weapon of praise brought a great victory.

Going back to Psalm 18:3, if you keep reading more of the following verses, you will see a similar result of victory after they praise. Read Psalm 18:6-14:

"In my distress I called to the Lord; I cried to my God for help. From his temple he heard my voice; my cry came before him, into his ears. The earth trembled and quaked, and the foundations of the mountains shook; they trembled because he was angry. Smoke rose from his nostrils; consuming fire came from his mouth, burning coals blazed out of it. He parted the heavens and came down; dark clouds were under his feet. He mounted the cherubim and flew; he soared on the wings of the wind. He made darkness his covering, his canopy around him—the dark rain clouds of the sky. Out of the brightness of his presence clouds advanced, with hailstones and bolts of lightning. The Lord thundered from heaven; the voice of the Most High resounded. He shot his arrows and scattered the enemy, with great bolts of lightning he routed them."

The whole chapter is super encouraging, describing the power of praise and what it does for us. I love how wonderful God is. When we praise, he literally comes and knocks out our enemies for us.

As our family grew, we taught our children the same power of praise. There were times when we would be driving down the road and we'd all be arguing from an atmospheric funk that hung over us. In that moment, one of us would say, "Kids, it's time to shout, 'Jesus!'" Sometimes they'd say, "Oh no…do we have to?" But then we'd get ready, and at the count of three we'd all let out a shout, "Jesus! Jesus! Jesus!" We'd sometimes roll all the windows down and shout out the windows until the atmosphere changed. We'd end up laughing hysterically and enjoying the moment, and usually the tension would vanish.

On another occasion, Heather and I were distraught as we had just moved to Vacaville and our finances were not doing well. Our hearts battled to be encouraged, and it seemed like one trial after another plagued us. As we were driving near Napa one day, we both knew it was time to shout. It had come to that. We were desperate and needed a breakthrough.

THE MEASURE OF WARFARE DETERMINES THE MEASURE OF PRAISE

I love what my friend Dan McCollam says. He says something like, "The measure of your warfare determines what the measure of your praise must be." Heather and I have learned how to radically and unashamedly praise God. So, we threw the windows open and shouted at the top of our lungs, "Jesus, Jesus, Jesus!" and radical praise spilled out of our mouths.

He always comes through, breaking us through barriers. Sometimes the breakthrough is inside us – in our internal atmosphere. Sometimes a tangible reward comes, such as a financial breakthrough or a relational victory where there had been challenges. Other times, he is stretching our muscles and the battle continues. He knows how much we can handle.

Even recently I experienced several months of atmospheric warfare. Things were just tense in the spirit realm, suspicions were high relationally, intimidation was all around, and even though I knew I hadn't done anything wrong, the battle still wouldn't let up. It's no fun when you are a feeler like I am and the enemy is at work in the environments you're in. I feel stuff in the spirit, like discouragement, tension and fear. But there is a way of victory for the feeler.

I had taken as much as I could take and knew in my spirit that because of the measure of the warfare, I had to release radical praise. I've learned that sometimes praise has to look foolish to actually cause a shift over your circumstance. "Foolish" acts of praise, done from the right heart posture, are seen as humility to the Lord. When you humble yourself, he often times lifts you above the enemy warring against you. In that moment, I went outside on a walk. I was done with the enemy having his way in my mind, emotions and the atmosphere of my house. Have you ever had tension in your home that just won't lift? Sometimes tensions are in relationships, and other times it's just looming over the house. This was one of those looming times. As I took to the streets for my walk, I began to praise. I didn't care who saw or heard me. I was desperate. I knew I had to be good and humiliated before the Lord. This had to be a sacrifice of praise.

Imagine this: I began to dance and twirl around as I jogged for several miles around the neighborhoods surrounding my house. I passed construction workers, moms walking with their children and men walking their dogs. I danced, sang, raised my hands, twirled, and even shouted in my desperate condition. I didn't care. Well, I cared but I didn't (you know what I mean). My desire to be liked and dignified wrestled against my greater desire to be free from the battle surrounding me.

I so desperately wanted him. But make no mistake, he can't be tricked in this moment. He knows when there is real praise coming up out of our hearts for him and when we are just trying to pull a trick out of our spiritual bag. Tricks do not work with God. Desperate and intentional praise does, however. He heard my cries, saw my praise and reached out to me in that moment, breaking me free of that two-month battle.

THERE IS ALWAYS VICTORY

Remember, there is always a victory to be had after the battle is over. For me, that week I had an opportunity to speak at a place I hadn't spoken at in a while. There was a lot of battle over that place and my connection to it. Without me trying to create an opportunity to speak, I was given several very significant moments to speak in that place, and it brought a major victory to those who were there. It was a victory that had needed to come for months. That was one reward for my battle – an opportunity to speak. Another reward was seeing the victories others had through my message.

God never gives us more then we can handle, but always provides a way out for us so we can remain victorious. He is always doing things for us in the battle. He is teaching us to persevere. One of the definitions of perseverance in the Greek is "joyful constancy." Scripture says that when we learn to persevere, we'll have a reward. See it in Hebrews 10:36:

> *"You need to persevere so that when you have done the will of God, you will receive what he has promised."*

When we stay joyfully constant in the fight, we will certainly have a reward. We don't fight just to fight. Every warrior fights for a crown, a reward or the freedom that comes as a result of the battle. We, too, need to look forward to the rewards, our rewards, as we properly fight with perseverance (joyful constancy) the battles that come. Joy is a strategic part of our New Covenant battle weapons. Let's talk about how to wield your joy weapon for victory.

CHAPTER TWO

JOY WARFARE

My heart was endeared to the UK warriors who had given so much for our land. The cost they had paid did not go unnoticed. I made a vow in my heart that at some point, I would repay my UK warriors. I did not know how or when, but I knew that when the time was right I would do it. The answer to how I would do that came suddenly one day.

An acquaintance from the UK had a dream about me, causing him to hunt down my phone number from a friend. When he got on the phone with me, he shared his dream. In his dream I was going to the four high places in the UK and doing battle. There was something in the dream about the county of Kent and a few other details that I have since forgotten. Before he called, I didn't even know what the high places were, but quickly found out they were four mountains, one in each of the four nations of the UK: England, Wales, Scotland and Ireland. The mountains were Slieve Donard, Ben Nevis, Scafell Pike and Snowdon.

The dream was enough to give me the strategy I needed to know how to repay my UK family. I was excited, but I knew the way we played out the strategy would have to be different than the walk in Northern California.

We built a team and found the right time to travel to the UK. We were super excited and had called together a UK team to meet. With the team from the US and the team from the UK, at certain times we had up to 30 prayer walkers with us. When we got everyone together for the first mountain we were going to climb, we told everyone the strategy for the walk.

Some of the people joining us from the UK were seasoned walkers. More than three/fourths of our team were not, however. Those from the UK were used to battle, and we were mostly young and zealous, but rather inexperienced. I had been prepping our team for months, encouraging them to build physical endurance by climbing hills and whatever was available where we lived. Nothing could really prepare us for a few of the mountains that took us between 8 to 12 hours to get up and down with the whole team.

THE STRATEGY OF JOY

The strategy was simple: climb the mountain with joy. That was it. No major warfare prayers, no repentance over land issues or nation sins, no serious intercession, just the weapon of joy. It was a bit hard for some of the folks to catch on to. "What? Just joy?" The goal was simply to enjoy one another, enjoy the Lord, have fun and make it to the top.

On the first mountain, those who were super athletic climbed to the top and were finished an hour and a half before the last people on the team finished. After the first day was over, we gathered together to strategize, and knew for the next mountain we had to walk to the top together. Together would be a much more challenging endeavor. There was a mix of very experienced walkers and very inexperienced.

The second mountain walk was started, and before we reached the base of the mountain, someone was complaining that their backpack was too heavy. Other problems arose with people complaining of physical pain. My wife Heather also got injured in one of her legs, but she never complained an ounce. She led the charge many times and fought till the finish. But others weren't as mature. These folks tested the character of those who were physically fit and itching to get to the top of the mountain.

Slowly, we learned to work together. Some carried two backpacks and others held back for the slower walkers to catch up. Slowly, we were becoming a team. That was another layer to gaining victory in the Spirit in this walk.

One morning, as we walked to the base of the mountain to start our way up to the top, there was an earthquake. Not just any old earthquake, but actually the largest earthquake in 50 years for the specific area we were in. The earthquake happened the exact moment our feet touched the bottom of the mountain. The shockwaves went all the way to the county of Kent, causing some minor damage to several structures in that area. Remember the person from the UK who called me about their dream; the dream that launched our walk? Kent was in that dream. I didn't know the significance of Kent or even where it was located initially.

On a side note, 15 years later I connected with some prophet intercessors in the county of Kent who remembered the earthquake. I had the opportunity to release some significant strategies to them which have helped them move forward in seeing the county of Kent come into greater Kingdom purpose.

As we continued to walk the mountains, we did our best to maintain joy and enjoyment of each other. Another sign followed our time there. We were there in the month of April, and the whole time we walked the sun was shining. The news declared that during the month of April it was the most days of sun they'd experienced in 350 years. Coincidence? I think not. As we pressed into what God was saying about that sign, we sensed him say, "The sun (Son) was shining over the UK again!"

We finally made it to the final mountain, which was in Ireland. That mountain was actually a rather small climb compared to the other three mountains. We spent a week or so in the area before getting to our last climb. As we neared the top of that last mountain/hill, several people in the group started emotionally falling apart. I was learning some things about warfare at that time, and knew that relationships were where the breakdown can occur in battle. I'll touch more on this in a later chapter.

We worked through those issues, and then walked together to the top of the mountain. We walked the last several hundred yards arm in arm with one another, and when we hit the top of the mountain, most of us burst supernaturally into tears. This was a joy walk, but we ended in tears. Coming from America, we really had no idea how much devastation had been wielded in that country against one another. Numbers of people had lost their lives in the internal war of that nation. Bombings, killings and devastation were real issues for many years there.

That night, after we walked down off the mountain and into the city, we met a man in the city who had killed several people and also had loved ones killed in the internal division in that nation. We led him to Jesus and to receive forgiveness for what he had done. We also helped him pray to forgive what others had done to him. The next day, another sign occurred. For the first time in 40 years, the country had two opposing political parties create an agreement to work together. Coincidence again? You decide.

Now, were we the big champs who caused the major breakthroughs and the signs and wonders in the UK? No. We played a very small but still significant part in the victory of that nation. Many years and thousands of prayers and effort had been already in play by many others. God graciously taught us the power of joy and unity to bring his Kingdom to a nation in the form of healing divided political parties. He caused nature to respond to the joy we operated in and the unity of two different nations' prayer groups: the UK and America. Nature responded with unusual sunshine and an unusually sizable earthquake for that area.

Joy is very powerful. Joy is a huge part of the nature of God. In fact, joy is one-third of the Kingdom of God. Romans 14:17 says, "The Kingdom of God is not a matter of eating and drinking, but of righteousness, peace, and joy in the Holy Spirit."

God's very presence is known by joy. NKJV says in Psalm 16:11, "In his presence is fullness of joy."

JOY IS A MORE POWERFUL WEAPON THEN FEAR

I like to say that New Covenant people are to be known by how much joy they get about the finished work of Jesus. If you watched the Disney movie *Monsters Inc.,* you'll get a good illustration of the power of joy to create life instead of fear's limited power. In the movie, when monsters frightened children, they captured an energy source to power their city, not realizing there was another way. So often we think that warfare is all about being the most vicious, the most aggressive, the most assertive against the enemy. In *Monsters Inc.,* they spent the whole movie trying to be masters at scaring children. But in the end, they discover that laughter and joy actually did much more to bring power to the entire city's energy needs.

Just look at a very clear strategy on dealing with the enemy found in Psalm 2:4-5:

> *"The One Enthroned in heaven laughs. The Lord scoffs at them.*
> *He rebukes them in his anger and terrifies them in his wrath."*

What is this most powerful weapon? Laughter. Laughter is one of the core foundations of joy. I like to say that joy is like a chair that has four legs. One of the four legs of joy is laughter. The other three are praise, thanks, and testimony.

I remember a prophetic act/trip my Vacaville Emerging Prophet school went on. We were revisiting the five different locations our state capitol had been at over the duration of the State of California. One of the locations was San Jose. We went to where the state capitol used to be. There isn't a state building there anymore – just a memorial engraved into the concrete in the place where the capitol once was.

When we got there, I noticed a lady who looked homeless sitting there. I tried to talk to her, but she wasn't responsive. So, we went about praying and doing our prophetic act in that location. In our prophetic act, we prayed in a circle, declared things, walked in a circle one direction and then switched and walked in the other direction. All of these acts, as well as a few others, were significant in moving towards the breakthrough God intended us to have that day.

After we had been praying a while, that same lady, who I had tried to talk to earlier, started to cuss at the top of her lungs. She cussed and cussed and cussed. One of the intercessors saw a demon perched on the top of a building next to where we were instigating things in the Spirit. The cussing didn't stop, and we continued to pray and do our prophetic acts.

Nothing changed and the atmosphere got thicker and thicker with oppression. I was feeling the heaviness and decided that maybe we should just move around the corner to get away from that level of vileness. As we began to leave, one of our seers fell to the ground and started to laugh very loudly. He laughed and laughed and laughed. I didn't get into it and wasn't feeling any sort of joy at that moment. I was emotionally worn out by the cursing that had gone on and on.

LAUGHTER BROKE INTIMIDATIONS GRIP

As he laughed, others started to join in. He wasn't laughing at the lady or being disrespectful at all. He was just doing what sometimes must be done. He had entered into the laughter of God at his enemies. As he did, the lady quieted down and the spirit over that area broke.

Suddenly things changed. Two of our Emerging Prophets went over to the now silent lady and asked to pray for her. For the first time since we were there, the lady responded with a, "Yes," and allowed them to pray for her. When they were done, she left the area. The battle had been won through joy. I asked the seer intercessor later why he burst into laughter. He said that the spirit that was assaulting us was intimidation and that he wasn't going to let that spirit have his way. Thank you, Jesus! What a valuable lesson to learn. Joy is so powerful for the New Covenant believer.

When we laugh and rejoice, we are entering into God's victory. We are remembering what he has done for us. We find strength in this joy. Nehemiah 8:10 says, "The joy of the Lord is your strength." Joy is a strategy that releases the strength needed to win battles. If you think joy is for wimps, think again.

Coming home from the joy walk in the UK, it wasn't too long afterwards that I decided to do a joy walk in our region. We planned a week-long journey of walking through seven cities, from several hours north of us all the way to the southern border of our home city, Willits. I had this prayer walk planned for some months, but I didn't have the specific details of the strategy of the walk until right before the walk started. I share more specifically about this walk in my book, *The Happy Prophet*.

A mentor knew I had been struggling with fear, and so he told me that in order to break the spirit of fear, I needed to take the jesters hat (I had bought in the UK) and wear it during the entire prayer walk through the seven cities we were going to walk through. I wrestled with the thought of it, but knew it was right. I needed to break a spirit of fear over my life and joy was the way to do it. Joy looked like foolishness in that moment, and I knew that God resists the proud, but gives grace to the humble (James 4:6). Sometimes humility looks like wearing a jester's hat.

INTERCESSION IS WARFARE

My greatest fear was now knowing that I had to do an intercessory walk with joy. Intercession is warfare. When you think of intercession, you don't usually think of joy; you think of seriousness and tears. There definitely is a place for those, but the key is to listen to the Lord's strategies. His strategies shift with different situations and circumstances. The walk definitely broke me free of fear, and I had my moments of being scorned and even cursed at. In this prayer walk, intercession looked like joy. Joy was the key that destroyed the enemy and brought victory.

Joy breaks religiosity. In one of the cities we walked into, there was a hostile takeover of the joyful prayer meetings we were hosting. The local pastors didn't like the joy and were offended at us. They later told us they were even jealous of us because we reminded them of the fiery people they used to be. I wasn't going to release the joy rebelliously in a church that didn't want it, but that night God hit me with such joy in the bathroom! Imagine the ridiculousness...I crawled out of the bathroom and to the stairs of the church meeting, and people had to walk near or over me to get into the meeting hall. Later on, some of the leaders of that church asked me to pray that they'd receive the joy I carried. Ridiculous joy is contagious.

Yes, joy is contagious, and joy is also an anecdote for offense. Bitterness is another word for offense. You can either be bitter, which is kind of like eating sour lemons, or you can be filled with joy, which is like partaking of honey. If you are feeling the bitter assaults of the enemy when you choose to be joyful, you are taking the medicine needed to keep that root of bitterness from growing internally inside of you. That is why Scripture says when people persecute you for righteousness, you are to rejoice (Matthew 5:12). Rejoicing will keep you sweet. If you don't learn to be thankful for those who don't receive you, you'll catch the rejection being hurled at you by those who oppose the Gospel and find yourself partaking of that same offense. You'll now be offended at those offended at you. At that point, you've lost the battle instead of defeating the enemy with the heavenly weapon of joy.

I'm surprised at how some people want to hold onto joylessness. When my wife or my kids and I have had a disagreement that has caused us to lose love and kindness towards each other, we are in a standoff. There is a disagreement that is getting us nowhere. Sometimes another brilliant conversation explaining your point of view in that moment is not going to help. When we can tell there is a battle trying to divide our hearts from each other, laugher is needed. One of us has to make a choice to simply turn on laughter. We are not laughing at each other, we are simply laughing at the situation and how it has caused irrational distrust to break out between us, sometimes over the silliest of disagreements.

I love when joy wins in an argument. After the moment of laughter is when we sit next to each other, wondering what it was that we were fighting about anyways. It certainly wasn't worth the tension.

Sometimes that's the nature of a battle. It spirals out of control with one person getting more and more hurt, and then they release hurtful words to the other person. That person then gets hurt and returns the words with more painful words. That is what warfare looks like at times. Warfare is won or lost many times around relationships, but relationships are definitely worth fighting for.

CHAPTER THREE

WARFARE IS NINETY-FIVE PERCENT RELATIONAL

———

I learned this powerful lesson years ago concerning warfare: warfare is 95% relational. Ephesians 6:12 says, "For our struggle is not against flesh and blood but against the rulers, against the authorities, against the powers of this dark world and against the spiritual forces of evil in the heavenly realms." Sounds pretty clear to me. We are not fighting against people. But I've learned that the enemy always finds a way to make the battle relational if we are not healthy relationally. Sometimes we are healthy relationally, and the enemy still tries to take the battle that direction.

I shared in the last chapter about us taking a team to the top of the four high places in the UK. On the last mountain as we neared the finish line, people started to break down. One person said, "I'm not going to the top because you're a mean leader." Another person said, "I'm not going any farther because nobody cares about me." I stopped the team and, in that moment, with confidence in my heart, said, "Guys, this is warfare 101." You see, I had been learning about the connection between relationships and warfare for a few years. I also told them that I was committed to not going any farther up the mountain until they were healed and went up with us. We stayed in that spot for at least 30 minutes until the two that had gotten stopped by unhealed wounds finally got healed, then we were able to walk up the mountain together.

One of the things I had learned while pastoring was that you could open the heavens through worship, the supernatural and the prophetic, but if you didn't have relational health in the leadership and the congregation, then the heavens would close right up again.

I have seen this lesson repeat itself over and over again in many nations and on many trips. Many times, I had watched people excitedly think that they were going to go bring a big change to another church, another city or another nation. What they didn't realize is that in the strategic moment of victory, the enemy would begin to trigger the unhealed, festering wounds and hurts that were unchecked beneath the surface.

UNDERSTANDING THE ENEMIES STRATEGY WILL HELP

In the critical moment of battle, the enemy touched the point of rejection, suspicion, bitterness, hurt, or whatever other pain is there to knock out the warrior. The one who is supposed to bring the victory has now been knocked out of commission. If there is a spot in your heart that is unhealed, it will be revealed in the moment of battle or right before a victory can be had.

I remember getting ready for the prayer walk in our region. The day before, I had a lady who had been festering with hurts unbeknownst to me, suddenly want to have a conversation with me before church started. She came into the church and found me greeting people at the door. She came straight for me and told me she was leaving the church. Her reasons? It was my loud praise that I dared to release in my neighborhood or anywhere in public. It was "inappropriate," and she would have nothing to do with it.

In reality, it had nothing to do with my radical praise. She had gotten hurt somewhere else, but wouldn't share what the real hurt was. Only later did other members of the church tell me her real offense, which I had no idea about. So, she lodged her offense dagger at my praise, then walked right out and left the church for good. I, on the other hand, was there with an invisible dagger in my heart as I had to emotionally try to pick myself up of the ground and lead the service that day, and then go out and lead the prayer walk that week. Thankfully, I had a spiritual father there who helped me see what was going on and gingerly pulled the dagger out of my heart through prayer and forgiveness, etc., from the lady who had hurt me.

You see, warfare comes at the least expected moment; the moment when you are expecting victory. Warfare most often looks relational because it gets you to get your eyes locked onto the offense, hurt, disagreement or maltreatment of yourself from another.

One time when my wife and I were still learning this principle about warfare, we had gotten ourselves locked into an argument that we couldn't get out of. We fought around and around it, about who knows what. Back then, it must have been important, but now I can't even remember what it was over. We weren't able to get out of the cycle of arguing and disagreeing. One of our intercessors had a dream about us being in this trick house where you never could get out. The doors always led you somewhere else in the house even though you wanted to find the way out. That was where we were: stuck in the house, not able to get free of our issues. She prayed for us and broke the cycle we were stuck in.

LEARNING TO WIN THE BATTLE

It took us a while, but eventually we started to learn how to win the battle. It started when we left our city and would drive over to Redding or Vacaville for a couple hours or a day. Either one of those cities was three or more hours away. Whether we went to Redding or Vacaville really didn't matter. The point was that once we left Willits and got out of the county we were in, we found ourselves really enjoying ourselves. We had great chats and many breakthrough conversations. But when we entered back into our city, before long we found ourselves in another cycle of disagreement. We finally began to recognize that our city had some battles in it that weren't ours.

One of the battles was in the area of mistrust. It caused a division in relationships. Our church also had years of small factions and splits through many pastors' tenures there. We didn't realize that we had the privilege of breaking through all of that funk to establish the new normal, healthy relationships.

There have been other times when we are going somewhere to do a significant prayer strike, prophetic act or even a weekend trip as a family to minister in a certain city. I remember when we took a team of people to San Francisco for one of several prophetic acts we did there. Our kids were with us and they were acting up. I was supposed to be leading the charge in this prophetic act, but needed to learn a valuable lesson along the way. What was more important than having some great prophetic act? My family's health. I turned my attention to my family and determined in my heart that the goal of that day wasn't some profound prophetic act or even engaging with the team. The real goal was to love my family well. As I did that, the battle diminished. When I made my family the focus instead of secondary, then things changed.

I've seen over and over again how people, ministers, businesspeople, you name it will sacrifice their family for the success of their mission. The mission might seem like the battle, but the real battle is over the family. You can win the supposed battle but lose the war if your family isn't loved well.

A wise prophetess told Heather and I that when she was getting ready to engage in some ministry trip or prophetic act, etc., that she had to remind her children about what would start happening. She'd have to remind one of her kids that when the spiritual climate dialed up, he'd start feeling rebellious. We've had to do that as well. It doesn't always completely eliminate the battle, but it certainly helps.

In the heat of the battle, we can all be on our defenses when we feel the tension in the air. Suspicion can soar in those moments, and the tendency is to think the people who we love and care for are the enemies. The enemy has a great way of twisting things around. Recognizing his tactics in those moments is very helpful.

Another time, Heather and I were getting ready to lead our church on a prophetic act through our city. Our city was known for a famous horse named *Seabiscuit*. Unbeknownst to us, on the very day we were doing our prophetic act through the center of town, there were famous people at our city theater to watch the first showing of the movie Seabiscuit. It was a significant moment for us to be doing a prophetic act. We were to be walking through our town waving banners, playing instruments, singing and dancing. The town of Willits was only 6000 people, and so when you do something like that, most likely other people in town will recognize you and comment on things later. It can raise insecurities in you, but also, it's a great way to shift the city atmosphere or break any personal fears you may have.

FIGHTING LIKE CATS AND DOGS

That particular morning, as Heather and I got ready and began to drive down to the starting point of that prayer walk, we were fighting like cats and dogs. We were locked into another battle, still not fully recognizing it as warfare. We fought all the way to the starting point of the walk, and then had to get out of the car after shredding each other to smithereens with hurtful words. I'm not even sure what we were arguing about, but I'm sure there was a lot God was trying to bring up internally in us; things that needed healing. In the moments where we are getting ready to take territory, watch closely. That is when the enemy seeks to destroy. Imagine having to lead a prayer walk after feeling guilty over hurting your spouse and also hurting from whatever your spouse said to you. Thankfully the prayer walk did end well and there was spiritual victory, and through the battle we learned a little more about what spiritual battle looks like.

My wife and I really do have a great marriage. We've been married for 22 years now. But I've learned that a great marriage doesn't mean you don't ever disagree. It just means you learn to work things out and how to love your way through those hurtful moments. You learn to get better in times of tension so you don't hurt each other like you used to. When the tension of a situation rises or the enemy brings warfare your way as you prepare to do something new in the Kingdom or take some territory in the mountains of influence, you learn to trust the people around you.

I always come into new territories with humility, because I know that there may be things in me that I don't see. I know if I come in humbly, then God will cover me. I know if I come in arrogantly and blindly thinking I am going to do some great work for God, I could be in for a relational lashing.

Often times we want to come into a new territory and bring heaven. First, we need to become more aware of the relational dynamics that surround the situation. Paying better attention to how much relational strength we have with people will certainly help us do better in the fight.

I recently had an exciting opportunity: hosting a conference in another city besides my own. Since I wanted to get away from all of the atmospheric funk that surrounds a church when it is in transition, I picked another city to host the conference in. As it turns out, the other city had just as much relational growth opportunities and funk show up even before we got to the conference. The conference ended up great, but I knew its success would be determined by my ability to navigate challenging conversations and misunderstandings. It takes a lot of wisdom to not let offenses and hurts knock you out of the game. We all get hurt and offended from time to time, but if we don't learn to get over things quickly, we won't be able to advance God's Kingdom.

OFFENSE FREE

It's not about never getting offended; it's about not allowing offense to grow up and become a bitter root that defiles many. As an example, the Lord told me he had a move of God for me to be a part of with some other leaders, but we would only see that move of God if we were in covenant with each other. He helped me see how we were not in strong enough covenant with each other at that time. For several years now, I have worked very hard to keep my heart in covenant with local leaders as well as other leaders who I am called to work with. The goal of this season, relationally, has been to hold the covenant even when in disagreement.

In another situation, one of my good friends and I have had some very serious disagreements as we have learned to walk together in the Kingdom. I heard the Lord say that I was in a 100-day test. When he said it, I didn't know in what way I was being tested; I just knew I was in some kind of test. As the 100th day approached, I suddenly became aware that the test was over the connection with my friend. We had some big disagreements in that time period, but we chose the covenant of friendship over the right or wrong of our views. We broke through the disagreements and found that our love for each other and friendship was stronger than our different views. As we continue to journey together, we've learned to give and take better. We have now been entrusted with being a part of what some would say is a move of God.

I'm so thankful the Lord has taught me that relationships are what the fight is really over. If you are alone at the end of the day, you have not won. Elijah was alone and could not win the national victory that was needed. He needed family and he didn't have that. He had to anoint Elisha who was much better at family. It was Elisha who commissioned one of his spiritual sons in the company of the prophets, who then anointed Jehu, who was the one to finally take out Jezebel. Jezebel was the enemy of true family. You can't take out Jezebel as a loner. Elijah was a loner, and so he couldn't take her out. He could start the revolution, but it took a son with a family mindset to complete it.

If we are to begin to see the nations turn back to God and the kingdoms of this world become the kingdoms of our God, then we need to understand the importance of family and relationships. God's mandate is for us to disciple nations once we get healthy relationally, and then we'll begin to see the nations come to him in greater measure.

CHAPTER FOUR

BEFORE YOU HAVE AUTHORITY IN A NATION, THAT NATION WILL TEST YOU

———

Often times we get excited to go to another country, church or city to bring the Gospel. Feelings of grandeur capture our hearts in those moments, and we can feel like we are getting ready to make a big difference. One of my leaders told me years ago, "Keith, we are not the great white hope." I knew what he meant: stay humble. Now, that was not a prejudice statement, rather it was a statement telling me that wherever I went, I wasn't there to be the big answer just because I was American, a preacher, a prophet, or anything else, even the color of my skin.

I have loved one of the values of The Mission Church in Vacaville that I have been a part of for 11 years now. They call it "strategic life exchange." It means that wherever I go, I am there to learn some things and also to give some things. Yes, giving is important, but it is only half the equation. Paul said in Philippians 4:15, "Not one church shared with me in the ministry of giving and receiving, except you only."

One 30-year veteran missionary told me, "Keith, I have a truth to tell you. One that people think is a heresy." She said, "I tell missionaries whenever I am training them that God sent them to that country because he thought it would be a good way for him (God) and them to get to know each other." Often times missionaries will go somewhere because they feel they have a great mission to go on to reach the lost people they are being sent to. That may be a secondary purpose, but it is not the primary one.

Why am I taking the time to set this up this way? Because sometimes when we go somewhere to take territory, we have to realize that certain internal characteristics protect us and certain ones hurt us. When we go thinking we are going to do some *great work* somewhere, we may set ourselves up for a fall. If we do, we might be blindsided by the enemy in those moments. That attitude can quickly make us fall into pride. When I take a team to a different country, I will tell them that they are not just there to bring or do some great thing. They are there to receive some things from the locals.

I remember taking a team to the far away island of Vanua Levu, Fiji. We were going to be met there by some of the local Fijians who were a part of our supernatural schools from the main island, Viti Levu. They had taken a boat to get to where we were, and we had flown many hours to get there. When we arrived, we had our first meeting at a church. I immediately had the Fijians start off the church service not just with worship, but with prophetic ministry and signs and wonders. They began to stir up the Spirit of God, and before long, miracles were flowing. They began to stretch the people's faith; the people who came from the States. These were the ones coming to make a great impact, right? But the folks from the States were being impacted. We had come to do the ministry, but were being ministered to.

I rested back in my chair as I watched the beautiful site of the locals teaching us about the things of the Spirit. I thought to myself, "The Kingdom of God really works. We came to help build a school here a few years ago, and now here they are teaching us some things about the supernatural." That posture of humility and Kingdom life exchange will protect you wherever you go.

PROTECTED WITH HUMILITY

I understand now that when I come into a nation, I must walk in humility. If there is a stronghold in that nation or region, I will first get tested with that stronghold. Only when I have an authority in whatever it tests me in will I be able to make a Kingdom impact there. I remember the first time I learned this valuable lesson about national warfare. It was during my first time visiting England.

Previously, I had wanted to travel oversees to Pakistan. I was invited and I was to be preaching on a large stage with thousands of people. How exhilarating, right? But looking back, I realize it wouldn't have been the right foundation for my international future. God knew I needed a much smaller relational foundation to start with. So, I went to England first. I actually went to England with only a three-day notice.

My good friend's wife had passed away. She was the one who passed away nine months after the prayer walk. The two of them had been with us on the California prayer walk. With short notice, I went over to be there for my friend at his wife's funeral. The one piece of advice I received in prayer from my American intercessors was to keep my mouth shut. That was a lifesaver. I was very surprised at the different way of thinking that was present in the people I met from my first international trip oversees. It wasn't about who was right or wrong, it was just different. They had different views on politics, different views on drinking alcohol, different views on church, and very different views on America.

I'm a patriot, and so hearing the different views on politics and America jolted me. But I was thankful for the word I received on keeping my mouth shut. I learned a lot that trip. My world view was slowly being expanded. It made me realize I had such a small-town view of the world. Well, I guess it made sense, since I had lived in Willits for almost 20 years, a town of 6,000! I was thankful I was getting a larger view of how people in the world think and what mindsets they operate from.

One of the things that surprised me most was when I went home, I struggled for several months afterwards with shame. Shame accelerated in that season and was pounding me from all sides. I cried out to one of my mentors asking them what was going on with me. They said it was actually a good thing. "The nation of England has a struggle with shame, and because you went there, the shame that was hidden in you got triggered so you could get free of it."

You see, I was still on my journey of coming out of religion. Guilt was normal for me. Shame was a friend. I thought the voice of shame and guilt was the Holy Spirit. At that time, my journey was to receive the unconditional love of the Father. That trip accelerated my journey to get free of the bondage from the shame and guilt I'd carried for so long.

THE ANECDOTE FOR THE DARKNESS

Later, I went back several times to the UK. The joy walk was a part of that. What we brought to the UK was joy; joy that came from knowing I was loved unconditionally and that the Father was pleased with me. That joy was the anecdote for the dark, religious funk that hung over the UK. In a small way, we were able to shed some light in that land, or maybe just amongst the ones we related to. They greatly impacted us, and we had some impact there too. That is what sustainable, Kingdom work looks like. Humbly bringing what you carry, but first learning about a culture by tasting of its fruits, good, bad or ugly.

I saw and experienced this principle over and over again, until I realized this was a Kingdom strategy for sustainable warfare. Go into a church, region or nation, and after a few days you can begin to recognize what the spirit over that location is. If that demonic spirit has any holds in you, there will first be a testing in you to get you free. Only then will you be able to bring an impact.

Surprisingly, the best way to bring an impact is by not directly confronting that spirit, but by walking in the opposite spirit. However, you can only walk in the opposite spirit if you actually carry the breakthrough inside of you. Prophetic people can only speak about something they are congruent with inside. Teachers can sometimes teach concepts that they have not mastered yet, but for a prophetic person to bring impact, they have to *become* the message. That is why you have to humbly come. If you don't humbly come, you will easily be defeated.

I kept learning this lesson in other nations. I went to Fiji and had a great time there seeing the people of Fiji embrace the supernatural. Everywhere we went signs and wonders followed the people who we trained. They learned that miracles indeed worked through their hands. At the end of the summer of living in that island nation, I told the Lord I loved the schools that we were a part of planting, but the poverty spirit I had to deal with regarding the finances of the school made me not want to be a part of it again. He said, "Good, then I need to get that same poverty spirit out of you!" (For more about this story and getting free of a poverty mindset, read my book, *Unlocking an Abundant Mindset*.)

You see, I had some positive impact in that nation, but then that nation helped start me on a new journey: the journey to get free of poverty. That journey took ten years. Sometimes we want to impact places in a very quick and easy way, but in reality, it could take years to get us ready to truly be the prophetic voice who can be the message, not just speak the message. The best way to get rid of territorial spirits is to become a new territorial spirit. Become filled with God's Spirit; his Spirit that is uniquely built into you as the answer to the problem in that region.

LEARNING HOW TO DEAL WITH
THE ELDER BROTHER SPIRIT

Once again, I went to another nation. I was in a season of traveling to numerous nations: Singapore, South Korea, Philippines, South Africa, Denmark, Fiji, and England. I went to South Korea and took a close armor bearer with me. He had partnered with me for years in the States. I had no idea what was about to transpire with bringing him with me to this nation.

As soon as I entered South Korea, their culture of honor showered on me. I was treated with dignity and honor and was given many accolades. It's a part of their culture – they honor guests well. But what transpired was that honor provoked jealousy in my armor bearer. Instead of him being a support to me, he became a wall of offense. He was supposed to be praying away demonic spirits, but instead he was inviting them with his bitterness towards me. It's true that we had some history and maybe there were hurts in our relationship that hadn't been worked through yet. But now that we were going to try to minister on a higher level, they were being exposed. Instead of me having a glorious ministry trip, I had to preach around 30 messages in ten days, minister prophetically to hundreds of people and sleep in the same room with my armor bearer who was opposed to me the entire trip.

BEFORE YOU HAVE AUTHORITY IN A NATION...   **49**

During that trying time I learned a lot. I did my best to honor my armor bearer and find ways to show him he was valuable. I was trying to bring the jealousy down, but it wasn't working. In that moment, there was nothing but mistrust. If you want to deal with a spirit such as that, you have to understand the spirit and how it works. An elder brother spirit (like the Prodigal son's older brother) is like the spirit that came over Joseph's brothers to the point where they could say nothing nice about Joseph. They hated him. Joseph was also a part of that same spirit when he boasted about his dream concerning his family bowing down to and serving him. He provoked the spirit of jealousy, and it threw him into a pit. Of course, God can turn even what the enemy meant for evil into something good, and he did in that situation!

But I didn't seem to get much breakthrough in my situation while on the trip in South Korea. It took about six months for that particular relationship to get back to normal. When you bring a relationship into a nation, it will certainly test it if you have some underlying lack of health. I still had a way to go to learn how to deal with the elder brother spirit. This situation was several years before I learned some significant keys to help me overcome that spirit when it manifested in people.

One of the keys I have learned since is that when someone is competing with you for attention, instead of sharing more stories about yourself, turn your attention to their stories. Get a genuine heart for what they are achieving, then affirm the heck out of them and turn the attention away from you. As I've learned to champion insecure spiritual brothers and friends, God told me one day that he had been building a father's heart in me. He said, "In becoming a champion of your brothers, I've been building a father's heart in you." Amazing and profound that in the caring for your peers you can grow a father's heart.

We might assume that to grow a father's heart, we should be caring for sons. But with God, his ways are different. All that to say when a spirit is revealed that you can't overcome in a city or nation, it doesn't mean you won't overcome it. It just means you might have a journey to go on to really internalize the Kingdom breakthrough needed to carry that breakthrough inside of you.

YOU CAN DISCOVER PATTERNS
THAT TRANSFORM

Are you starting to see a pattern here? Do you recognize the spirit in the cities and nations you have entered into by how that nation's atmosphere affects you? One of my mentors says it takes about four days for what is over a city to begin to be recognized. If you go somewhere on a vacation, you may really enjoy it if you are only there a couple days, but if you wait a few days longer, you may begin to see what's really going on.

Some people get tired of where they are living, visit another location and have a glamorized view of that new location. They think it will be the best thing ever to get away from their current, challenging situation. The grass is not greener on the other side though. If I give something adequate time, I will see the real fruit of that situation. I'm not expecting to find bad everywhere I go, but I've learned I will see real life situations happening. The spirit of that area will eventually present itself, and it has different (but very real) challenges in it also.

It's kind of like the difference between dating and marriage, or the difference between the honeymoon and regular married life. Marriage is amazing, but it takes work. The honeymoon feelings do wear off and you do have to learn how to navigate each other's differences. That is a joy, but sometimes if you don't come into the marriage with a clear knowledge of what those differences are you can be in for a painful awakening.

I'm not sure how many times I've been around someone who feels ready to leave a boring or difficult town they've lived in for a long time. I'll tell them they can either get a horizontal promotion or a lateral promotion. A horizontal promotion means you actually accomplished the task God had for you in that first location, and the next location is going to be a place of greater favor. A lateral promotion means you'll move to another location thinking it will be better, but because you didn't pass the lessons you needed to learn in the previous place, the same character development issues will happen all over again to you in the new location. Different faces, same problems.

In assessing different locations and how to bring the Kingdom of God's victory to those places, we just need to be real with what is actually going on there. Going from city to city and discovering what God's redemptive purposes are for that city or nation is a wonderful journey. It's also helpful to be able to discover what the challenges are for that city or nation. So, beyond how an area's strongholds affect me, how else can we discover God's redemptive purposes for that place and its current challenges?

I received a lot of great insights on how to recognize different city types from a prophet friend of mine named Martin Scott. He taught me so much about recognizing how each city has parallels to one of the seven city types found in the first few chapters of Revelation. Since then, I am able to go into a city and see if it is an Ephesus-type or more of a Thyatira-type city, etc. I can usually see different characteristics of the 7 city types when I spend time in a particular city. Once I've pieced together enough of those characteristic pieces, I am usually able to deduct from that information what that city type is. The same goes for nations. I've learned how to recognize different characteristics in a nation to help me understand what that nation's redemptive graces are and what type of nation they are. Recognition isn't for the sake of judging that city or nation though, but for the sake of being able to correctly diagnose where they are now and where God wants to take them. It gives me greater understanding and a bigger picture from God's perspective.

We are called to serve cities, geographies and nations. Sometimes serving them looks like experiencing the demonic principalities they are wrestling with so we can identify how to help them get breakthrough from those strongholds. Once you've identified them, strategic prophetic acts can be done to bring breakthrough to the area. I've spent a lot of time doing prophetic acts, which involves diagnosing the climate over a city, then declaring God's redemptive purposes into that city. It's something I do, and you can too.

CHAPTER FIVE

PROPHETIC ACTS THAT ADVANCE HEAVEN'S AGENDA

———

Over the last five years, I've done at least 25 prophetic acts that involve the group of Emerging Prophets who I mentor. As you can imagine, I've learned a lot in those 25 acts. Seeing how each act is going to unfold is exciting. Let me share a few things I've learned.

The first five prophetic acts we did revolved around the five locations our state capitol was located at. Our capitol has been located in San Jose, Benicia, San Francisco and Sacramento twice. We would take the team to one of those locations every six weeks. When we went to San Francisco, I was all fired up. San Francisco is a super controversial place. Of course, if you have been in the body of Christ for very long, you've probably heard a few remarks lodged against San Francisco. If you've been in the prophetic streams, you've probably heard a few judgmental words against San Francisco as well. You've probably heard that another Bay-Area earthquake would come as a sign of God's anger. I've heard all sorts of things. I've even heard that all of California would drop off into the ocean. But what I teach my Emerging Prophets is different.

We do love spiritual exercises. I teach the students to first find love in their heart for a place like San Francisco. I teach them to go beyond just noticing and focusing on the negative that's obvious in a city. That's a good start: to see the negative and flip it. But I'd consider that level one in prophetic development. Level two is not even seeing the sins anymore.

LOVE BASED PROPHETIC ACTS

I challenge my students to think about how they would prophecy over a city like San Francisco if they didn't see its sins. Where would they start? We practice getting our love on for that city and declaring things like, "I love you, San Francisco, kiss, kiss, kiss." We even sometimes make kissing sounds to emphasize the emotion of love we are exuding towards that city. A prophecy that will truly impact a city can't be forced love, but real, felt love. It has to get to the place within you where you exude God's love and see his redemptive purposes for a city.

When you begin to get this level of love for a city, then you are ready to go into it and do a prophetic act. So, I took a team and we went in. We ended up visiting the location where the capitol had resided briefly in San Francisco. There is now a tall apartment complex where the capitol used to be. It doesn't even have an official seal or anything on the ground to show it is where the capitol once was.

I sensed the Lord say that whatever we did that day needed to be done from a place of honor. One person brought a trumpet, another brought a drum and I brought my shout. We decided to do some shouting, drumming and dancing around in that area. It wasn't too long before a nice security guard came and asked us to leave. As we left, I remembered what the Lord had said. Suddenly, I realized I had missed the right way to do the prophetic act. In my zeal to clear the spiritual air with worship, I hadn't paid attention to his strategy.

Deep underneath I was thinking, "I don't really care about you, San Franciscans. You know you are not walking morally before God." That made it easy for me to come in and blast away with the trumpet and shout, etc. I wanted to take dominion in the area and bring it back to God. Now, zeal is good when it is used in the right time and right place, but when you don't have love, it'll harm others and you too. I'm not happy to say those were my thoughts, but that day, that's where I was at.

I had spent a lot of time trying to get the lovey-dovey feelings going for San Francisco, but I still had some work to do. The prophetic act revealed a deeper level of love that needed to get into my spirit for this great city. Afterall, there may be some people in that city who truly are bound down by sin and carry an ungodly agenda, but there are a lot of other people who absolutely are set apart to God. I should have focused more on them. I have since then.

The day wasn't a complete wash. My wife brought some roses and gave them out to random strangers, telling them how valuable and precious they were. Some of them were very touched.

There isn't a one-size-fits-all approach to doing prophetic acts. You have to listen to God. Different cities call for different responses. In one city, we ended up at a university. The whole time was spent at the university. We were walking down the street, and suddenly it ended in front of two statues. These statues had very strange faces. As I stood between the statues, a terrible, evil feeling came over me. Despite that dark feeling, I knew it was a discernment and we were supposed to be right there.

As we prayed, we were looking for the right strategy. I don't believe we ought to just bind every spirit when we go somewhere. I think our understanding of the verse in Matthew 16:19, "Whatever you bind in heaven shall be bound on earth," needs an upgrade. I don't want to react to every speck of evil that I see. If I do that, I am really responding out of a defensive posture instead of a posture of a son of God; a son who has the authority of Jesus at his disposal.

BINDING AND LOOSING ISN'T A FORMULA

Binding and loosing doesn't always work. Have you ever just tried to cast random demons out of random people? Does it work to just go wherever, whenever, and cast demons out? Do you find they come out every time at the simple use of the name of Jesus along with the phrase "I bind you, devil"?

Now, there are definitely times when you need to say just that. "In Jesus name, I bind you devil." In the moments when he orchestrates that phrase, it is effective. Remember the disciples were trying to cast out a devil, and they found a certain one that could only come out with prayer and fasting (Mark 9:18). That warning goes for us too. The seven sons of Sceva also got an abrupt awakening when they tried to use the principle of the name of Jesus, whom Paul preached. They got trashed by the demon and sent away naked as we see in Acts 19:14-16:

> *"Seven sons of Sceva, a Jewish chief priest, were doing this. One day the evil spirit answered them, 'Jesus I know, and Paul I know about, but who are you?' Then the man who had the evil spirit jumped on them and overpowered them all. He gave them such a beating that they ran out of the house naked and bleeding."*

They had a principle, but weren't yielded to Jesus and known by God. That cost them their dignity and taught them a very embarrassing lesson.

When I am near something like the statues during a prophetic act and feel an evil presence, I want to stay long enough to know what God wants me to do about it. There are so many possibilities God might lead me to. In this situation, he wanted me to begin to worship. We began to focus our attention on God's goodness. We could tell what the spirit was, but we began to move in the opposite spirit. Eventually, the evil presence in that area lifted. Then we went on and found another statue. It, too, had an evil spirit connected to it. Not all statues do by the way, but these did.

Through the course of the next couple hours, we walked by several statues. We begin to bless what God was doing and speak to the destiny that God wanted to release in the education systems of California. A prophetic word began to bubble up about the schools being what would lead the way to a harvest in California.

As we continued, we began to call for students to come into the Kingdom. That very night, a meeting was going on in the city with one of the churches we are connected with. They had a bunch of random and unexpected college students come to their church that night. Never before had they ever had that many come. Some of them were impacted and got ministered to and even saved. That was definitely a small seed of breakthrough to what we had just prayed into.

LOOK FOR THE SMALL SIGNS

One of the things to become aware of regarding prophetic acts is to look for the small signs that breakthrough is happening. If not, you may not be encouraged to continue in these sort of spiritual warfare methods. They are effective though, when done with God's direction. Every time we have done a prophetic act, we have felt resistance, and then a breakthrough. Sometimes the breakthroughs were massive and very noticeable, and other times they were more subtle. But each one of them is important. If you want to get authority in a region, doing strategic prophetic acts is one way to do that.

Each year in our school we will do prophetic acts connected to what we feel is strategic during that time frame. One year, we felt we were to retrace revival hot spots in the region. We discovered that there was a revival hotspot in a rougher area in our region: in the city of Stockton. The hot spot was a fairgrounds where a revivalist used to host meetings years ago. You could tell the area had an unsettledness in the spirit. For some students, there was a bit of fear around being in that sketchy part of the region. A couple local intercessors joined us as well.

As we walked around the fairgrounds, we begin to get God's strategy for that area. We ended up discovering in the Spirit the revival's well and the angel who had been standing by that well. The angel of healing was present and was massive. In that moment, I could feel the spiritual gifts that angel offered when you were in partnership with his assignment. A desire rose up inside of me, and I began to pray that I might receive some of the healing anointing from that angel.

The fear of the Lord immediately came upon me and he rebuked me. He said, "These people have had enough taken from them. This is not for you; this is for the people of this area."

I repented quickly of assuming I could have some of that anointing. During my journey into getting a deeper heart for California, I'd learned that the stronghold spirit of the state was greed. It had become clear to me if I was to have authority in California, I could not desire her things, even good things. I had to have a pure heart for her without motives of what I could get from her. This was another reminder of the important heartbeat of love I needed to have.

If we are to have an authority in regions, states, nations, churches, businesses, or cities, we have to make sure we are free of any negative spirits that area has in it. How do we recognize the spirits in the area without becoming focused on the devil? I think that when we have his heart for an area, he will show us what is going on because we care about him. It is care for him that leads us into dealing with the enemy. In that way, we are not living in a reactionary mode to what the enemy would like to continually keep us focused on: him. Instead we are focused on the Lord, and when we are, there are times we go places and our discernment of spirits kicks on.

Sometimes we get provoked to understand what is holding down his people. That is how he led me to discover the spirit over California. I had been going through a two-year journey of trying to understand the meaning of the number 58, which kept presenting itself to me. At the end of several years, he showed me that California has 58 counties, which I didn't know. With this revelation, I knew he was giving me an authority and a mandate for California.

As I pressed in deeper, I began to ask what the principality was over our state. I thought surely it would be Jezebel or lust or something of that nature. I didn't expect for him to say greed. Once I researched it out, it made sense. Jezebel, lust and other spirits are all byproducts of greed. I found in several passages in Scripture that when it talks about greed, lust and impurity also surrounds those verses. For example, notice what it says in Ephesians 5:3-5:

> *"But among you there must not be even a hint of sexual immorality, or of any kind of impurity, or of greed, because these are improper for God's holy people. Nor should there be obscenity, foolish talk or coarse joking, which are out of place, but rather thanksgiving. For of this you can be sure: No immoral, impure or greedy person—such a person is an idolater—has any inheritance in the kingdom of Christ and of God."*

The fruit that is evidently seen coming out of California is immorality, in all forms. But the root of that spirit is actually greed. You can see it in California's gold rush. It caused many to come here with greedy motives for their own gain.

Doing prophetic acts and going after seeing a region you have authority in come back to God can take time. As you do one prophetic act, more clarity comes. As you pray, you pick up another nugget. Slowly, a picture begins to form. As time goes on, you may begin to carry a prophetic word in your spirit for that region or nation, because you have now seen what is going on in that region and have the answer to what is going on.

As an example, over time, a picture concerning our destructive California wildfires started to form. Some of the worst fires in history have ripped through our forests and cities destroying 1000's of acres, many people's properties and some lives as well. At first, I wasn't fully engaged in the prayers for my region. I was living in thankfulness that the fires hadn't touched my city. I thought since they were out of my sight, then they could be out of my more serious prayer life too. One day, the Lord rebuked me with a verse from Jonah. Jonah 4:9-11 says:

> "But God said to Jonah, 'Is it right for you to be angry about the plant?' 'It is,' he said. 'And I'm so angry I wish I were dead.' But the Lord said, 'You have been concerned about this plant, though you did not tend it or make it grow. It sprang up overnight and died overnight. And should I not have concern for the great city of Nineveh, in which there are more than a hundred and twenty thousand people who cannot tell their right hand from their left—and also many animals?'"

JONAH DIDN'T CARE

He reminded me that Jonah didn't care for the people of Nineveh and told me, "Don't think that these fires can't touch you." He provoked me into a godly fear, showing me I needed to get my heart connected to this issue. After that, I took a two-year prayer journey concerning the fires of California.

On a side note, sometimes we get worn down because we see so many disasters on the news all around the world, all the time. Our hearts can grow weary of caring and our prayers can become calloused. I'm thankful when the Lord wakes us up in our spirits and reminds us of our mandate.

For me, I didn't really know what to do. I prayed and prayed for the fires and the victims and asked the Lord for strategies. Nothing came for two years. That's a long time to pray for a region, knowing you're supposed to, without getting answers. One day on the way home from a trip in Southern California, I was about 15 minutes away from home after a six-hour drive, and I finally heard the Lord say the first thing in two years about this fire situation. He said, "These fires are neither democrat nor republican." In that moment, I knew what was going on with these fires was not political. It wasn't about a government party or policy that God wasn't pleased with.

It wasn't about one political party's favor with the Lord verses his anger at the other political party. It brought a lot of clarity. It didn't solve the problem, but led me one step closer to what was going on. After that I asked him if there was an answer that our government could bring to the fires. That same day an invitation came, from a senator who is a believer, to be a part of something at the California Capitol. God is indeed leading us in these things.

I am a researcher. When God begins to show me a puzzle and how it fits together, I don't rest until the picture becomes clear. In the case of California, it is not a quick fix for me. I have hosted 50-day prayer and fasting times with Doug Addison and Lou Engle. I have traveled to many cities in California. I have prayer walked hundreds of miles in this great state. I have done many prophetic acts. I have walked around the state capitol many times, praying and prophesying over the state. Over the last couple years, God has even opened doors for me to go inside the state capitol and have the opportunity to prophecy over numerous senators and government workers. It is a great privilege to do so, and I've also been able to take other prophets in to minister prophetically inside the capitol. In all of this, I am still on the path of discovery for the keys for breakthrough in our great state.

One day, I had been invited to the capitol with a couple other, more well-known prophets and an apostle, as well as several more influential pastors in the state. We were meeting with a few state leaders (believers) to discuss God's heart for our great state. The strategy for California is always on my mind in those moments, and I am waiting for God to unveil greater clarity on how things can change in our state. As I was there, it all of a sudden became clearly evident that the spirit behind some legislation currently being passed in our state is an unclean spirit. Now, that might seem too obvious. Of course, all spirits that go against God are unclean, but I knew specifically what the Lord was referring to when he gave me that discernment.

An unclean spirit has a very foul motive. It wants impurity to cover everything. It wants to pervert sexuality and pervert the young generation. It wants to open up legislation that will actually create a greater demonic portal over our children by removing parental authority and godly leaders' authority over our children. It wants children's rights, but rights that are not in line with how God designed family. God has a design for family, and whenever legislation changes his design, there is a consequence.

Some say that government's role is not to legislate family. I disagree. I believe that government leaders are fathers and mothers. Even if they are not acting as our heavenly Father would have them act, they still fill the position of a role model. Even if they are indirectly a father, they still are defining gender and relationships. Their actions cause those under their authority to be validated in whatever they legislate. If they validate homosexuality, then it causes a greater sense of validation to those who don't have healthy fathers and mothers speaking Kingdom identity in their life. It opens up demonic doors of confusion over sexuality and gender, thus advancing hell's agenda.

Some would say, "Well, brother, the parents and the pastor are supposed to be the ones really raising up children in the ways of the Lord. Government has no authority over our children when the parents and the pastor are active." I would say technically that is true. Yes, I am responsible for my children's identity. I don't have total impact on them, but I can have a major influence in their lives if I use godly principles in raising them. But world leaders, political leaders, Hollywood leaders, media leaders, rock star leaders, sports star leaders, etc., all play a role as well. That is why it is my responsibility to get God's heart for the region, state and nation I live in and am called to impact. We can't just sit by and think somehow we are safe from the evils that are out there. We can't just say that because we don't have family directly impacted by the troubles of the world we live in, that the issues going on within that region won't affect us.

This was the attitude I had about the fires and this was not an attitude the Lord wanted me to have. He wanted me to do my part. I still don't know how much impact I am going to have in the state of California or in other regions. I am on a journey of discovery. This journey is a good one. I am enjoying the unfolding of revelation concerning the spiritual map of the areas I am called to influence.

Part of spiritual warfare is understanding the grids of the areas you are called to influence. Sometimes understanding is all that is needed. Other times, you have to take a more aggressive approach. There is a time to bind and loose.

CHAPTER SIX

WHEN SHOULD I BIND AND LOOSE?

———

In 25 prophetic acts or more, only one time have I commanded a principality to leave. You see, I learned in some of the earlier prophetic acts I shared with you that doing that without understanding of what God wanted me to do was very costly. God doesn't want us afraid of warfare, but he does want us wise in our use of spiritual weapons.

One Saturday, I woke up to get ready for a prayer walk with our Emerging Prophets. We were going to a city I knew well. He spoke clearly to me that morning that he was giving me apostolic authority. That is all he said. I didn't really know what that meant, but I was going to find out.

We made our way to the city where we were going to walk around. We were planning on walking around several of its neighborhoods and the city square. As we walked, we came upon a man who was yelling at anything and everything. We continued to walk, and then when we circled back to that area, there he was, still yelling. This time, there was now a standoff between this normal looking guy and a number of police. The middle-aged man was yelling at the top of his lungs and the police were trying to have a calming conversation with him.

As we came into that area, the spiritual climate was very tense. Fear was in the air, and there was uncertainty about what would happen. A few bystanders were around, and the group of 15 or so of us watched from a distance. We stood near a statue that was in the middle of a pool of water. The statue was standing upright, but as I looked at it, I saw in the Spirit that the statue actually bowed. Right then, I heard the Lord say it was time to bind the spirit in that area. I had never done that before. But since I heard the Lord tell me earlier, he had given me apostolic authority, I had the courage to do it.

THE RIGHT TIME TO BIND THE ENEMY

I gathered the group together and told them what we were going to do. While the man still was yelling and the police were beginning to move towards a hostile takeover if that man didn't stop, we quietly bound the spirit that was ruling there. We were all gathered around the statue, which I had seen in the Spirit bowing to the Lord. That was the first time I had done that at the Lord's command. We quietly, but with authority, declared the spirit in that area had to go.

Moments after, the man became quiet and walked off as if nothing had happened. The spirit of the area manifesting through that man was bound and left quietly. You see, I have learned that at times when you are dealing with a principality it will manifest in a person. It was the same principle I shared a few chapters before when we were in San Jose, when one of our intercessors began to laugh in the midst of the loud, endless cursing. All of a sudden, the cursing stopped as he laughed, and the tension in the air left. The same thing happened here, except this time we didn't laugh, we simply bound the spirit and it left.

There is not one particular formula for dealing with the enemy. James 4:7 says that we are to submit to God, resist the devil and he will flee. Our first mandate in any spiritual warfare is to submit to God. He may want us to rest and do nothing. He told the Israelites to be quiet for seven days and then shout. His ways are higher. There is not one formula that gets the enemy every time. I wish it were as easy as, "In the name of Jesus, I bind you, Satan," but it isn't. It doesn't mean that the things he asks us to do aren't simple. They are just things we are only able to do as we surrender to him and get his strategy.

When the man left the area after we had bound the area's spirit, we knew it wasn't enough to just get rid of the spirit. We had to fill it with something. Scripture says that when a strongman is bound, that it comes back and finds the house empty and in order, and comes back seven times stronger. Matthew 12:43-45 says,

> *"When an impure spirit comes out of a person, it goes through arid places seeking rest and does not find it. Then it says, 'I will return to the house I left.' When it arrives, it finds the house unoccupied, swept clean and put in order. Then it goes and takes with it seven other spirits more wicked than itself, and they go in and live there. And the final condition of that person is worse than the first."*

We have to make sure that whenever we evict the enemy, we replace him with God's kingdom. There has to be a "no vacancy" sign on the door when the enemy tries to come back. He needs to know there is no room for him to return.

We went to the park area where he and the police had their standoff, sat on the benches and began to raise our hands and quietly worship. The police were still standing there, and one of our team went over, and out of respect, told the police what we were doing. The police were fine with it, and before long they, too, left. We then stayed in that place until the intimidation in the air lifted and the glory of the Lord filled that space. Several of our students began to see things in the Spirit, and before long we were seeing God's strategy for the area and prophetic vision for what he wanted to do there.

LEARNING TIMING

There is a time for everything as it says in Ecclesiastes 3. There is a time to bind and a time to lose, a time for war and a time for peace. We need to learn when each of these times are.

As God continued to teach me about the power of apostolic authority, I visited a leader of a major revival movement of the past. He'd had words spoken over him about his death from a visiting prophet. I wouldn't say this was a very New Covenant approach, because the prophet had declared that in a certain period of time this man would die. It was around the time of my visit that the prophet had declared the leader was indeed going to die. When I heard what had happened to the leader, I was provoked. The Lord once again told me to use my apostolic authority.

I spoke over the man prophetically about his future and what God was going to do through him, and then I broke the curse off of him from the other prophet. Over the next several days, the man began to get better. The curse was broken, and the prophetic word injected fresh life into him where there was previously death. The man continues to live today several years after that encounter.

Whether we are dealing with regions or dealing with people, there are enemies to be dealt with. Sometimes those enemies have to be directly addressed and named. Other times, we simply move in the opposite spirit of the evil to break the back of that thing.

There are times when the enemy won't leave until you speak with authority. Because I spent so many years not understanding how spiritual warfare worked, my only tactic was to scream at the enemy and bind him. I've seen people do this, and it is often more of a desperate and unfaith-filled way of operating. This happens because we don't have understanding on how to win the fight against the enemy. We exhaust ourselves binding this and that spirit. We think the devil is behind every rock and that everything that happens is from the devil.

That is not a faith-filled way to live. I used to live that way, so God had to move me away from that form of dealing with the enemy. He was trying to teach me I was on the winning team, and when you are on the winning team, you are not always on defense. You have to play defense sometimes, but you know you are the one with the authority and you can win.

I had to learn how to win in my 11 years of pastoring in Willits. Willits was a place where you could not make it without being a warrior. You could not make it if you did not know how to use your spiritual authority. I remember the first time I encountered a demon. My Grandpa Lewallen had been teaching me about spiritual warfare and the casting out of demons, but I hadn't yet experienced this.

LEARNING DELIVERANCE

Then, one Sunday I preached a message on deliverance. I had never experienced a deliverance or witnessed a real-life demonic manifestation until that day. At the end of the message, I bound every demon in that building and commanded them to leave. Nothing seemed to happen. So, I dismissed the congregation and went outside to say my usual goodbyes as people went home. At the end of the goodbyes, a lady from our church came out and told me I needed to come inside...now.

Once inside, one of our congregants was snarling at me with a demon manifesting through her. I had never seen that manifest in her before, but armed with my grandfather's wisdom and the sermon I had just preached, I boldly moved towards her. I commanded the demon to leave. It didn't. I then spent the next five hours commanding every spirit I could think of to leave that lady.

I asked the demon questions. I asked the lady questions. I asked the demon what its name was. I commanded that spirit to leave again. It didn't seem to leave. After five hours, I was exhausted and so was the lady. We both hoped she was free, but I don't think she really was free. She continued to struggle after that with immorality and other sins. This was all I knew: bind the devil, tell it to leave in Jesus' name and it has to go.

That is a true principle, but over the course of the next few years in that city, I learned more through many different situations. There were times I had to tell things to go and they would go. Sometimes people would stand up in my congregation and try to take over the service. Sometimes it would be a drunk person who was allowing a demon to manifest through his drunkenness. My grandpa taught me that if they confronted you publicly, then you were to answer them publicly. So, I rebuked the man who was speaking out in the congregation and bound the spirit operating in him. He immediately slumped down in the chair and slept for the rest of the service. He didn't wake up till everyone else had left. I was slowly learning I did have some authority over the devil. I was also learning that sometimes no amount of shouting would get rid of the devil. Sometimes another ingredient was needed.

Once, late at night, I had a homeless person come to my door to ask for a blanket. I had one, and so I gave it to him. You see, we lived next to the church, and so we would have frequent "guests" visiting us whenever they needed something. When I gave this man the blanket, he proceeded to cuss me out and then leave with his blanket. I'm not sure what he was cussing me out for. He probably was demonized. But a few months later, he came back.

At this time, I was standing outside my church talking to someone. The man approached in a pleasant manner and asked for some help from the church. He spent time talking about how good of a guy he was and how he wanted to be able to stay in our church. He presented himself in a kind way as if he didn't remember what he had done before. He was being deceptive. I told him with an aggressive authority, "Get out of here right now, you deceiver!" I may have seemed a little too strong, because the person with me gave me a perplexed look.

Despite possibly being a little too tense in that moment, this town was teaching me that I needed to have authority and boundaries with people (and sometimes the enemy in them). The boundaries I was learning to have weren't mean boundaries or lack of love, rather they were a part of my journey of learning to deal with the enemy.

When you love someone, you fight for them. When you love a city or a nation, you fight for it. The enemy doesn't want that city or nation or even your church or family to breakthrough. There are times when you have to have strong boundaries.

Going back to the lady who I attempted to cast a demon out of, she stayed in our church for several years more. She had some open doors to the devil that she wasn't ready to close. She had numerous, sexually-immoral situations she would "find herself in" over and over again, despite professional counseling (which we offered her through a counselor at our church). She continued to say she was doing things God's way but would then slip into sin again.

ASKING SOMEONE TO LEAVE

After many times of dealing with her, I asked her to leave the church. It was extremely difficult to do, but I did it with my wife present to support me. It was so hard to tell someone they couldn't be a part of our church anymore. But when I finally told her, she pleaded for me not to do it. Even so, I told her she needed to go. As she left, the sky literally felt like it got bluer. There was a freedom that came over our spiritual climate.

Sometimes telling someone to leave is getting rid of spiritual darkness. They have chosen not to get free, and so there comes a time when you need to hand them over to the devil. In 1 Cor. 5:5 it says:

> *"Hand this man over to Satan for the destruction of the flesh, so that his spirit may be saved on the day of the Lord."*

Doing this is not something I enjoy, but I even had to learn this while youth pastoring. Some of our youth wrestled with choosing to do the right thing despite the many times I encouraged them in the ways of the Lord. One rebellious youth kept himself aloof from me and continually dabbled in pot, impurity and witchcraft movies.

One day at a youth retreat, I was preaching on revival. When I was done, he walked by me and I put my arm around him and asked him how he was doing. As soon as my arm went around him, he puked up a demon. He dramatically shouted out, "What just happened to me?!" He then thanked me over and over again, as he felt so much better after the demon had left. I told him, "You know, there are three doors you need to close or else that demon will come back. The doors of witchcraft, drugs and impurity." Sadly, he didn't listen and went back to his sin.

When a youth would get to that place, I would tell them straight up, "You are welcome to continue with whatever sin you are a part of if you are okay with a demon coming into you in the process." Of course, this was serious. They used to hate hearing me say that. "What do you mean? I'm going to get a demon if I do that? No, that can't be." In a sense, I was turning them over to the devil. Sometimes we need to bind the devil, and other times we need to let him kick the person around a little bit till they run off naked and can no longer hide their sin.

Sometimes warfare isn't so neat and tidy. People have lots of nice little ideas about Christianity. "Oh, Christianity is all about grace and mercy." I say yes, it is, for the obedient. But for those who choose to continually go against the grace of God, there are other ways God uses to get their attention. You can bind and cast out demons all you want, but if you are in agreement with a demon, no amount of binding will give you victory over that demon.

CHAPTER SEVEN

YOU CAN'T CAST OUT DEVILS YOU ARE IN AGREEMENT WITH

———

S everal years ago, I had been on a pursuit of resurrection power. I hadn't seen a resurrection from the dead, but I was provoked and wanted to see it. God had even shown me the date of when a friend would die and what I was to do when he died. I had no idea that he was near death and was out of cell phone range when I heard that from the Lord.

A few days later when I got back into cell phone range, I called and found out he was dead. I had a vision and the word of the Lord and knew I was going to get a resurrection that day. We took a team to go and pray for his dead body, over six hours away. Even though I had the faith, because the Lord gave me a word about this man in the midst of a ten-day fast I'd just come off of, we did not experience resurrection.

But that didn't stop me. I continued my pursuit of resurrection power by praying every chance I could for those who died. Since I worked for the local mortuary, when somebody died, often I would be on call and would have to go and pick up the dead body. There came a time when a mother lost her little baby. Of course, that was devastating, and I suggested I could go pray to see the child come back to life. My associate pastor and I went to the mortuary to do just that. I had the faith and the presence of God was also there. We prayed and prayed, but nothing happened. It was not pleasant to tell the mother her child wouldn't be coming back because we couldn't raise him from the dead.

That wasn't the end of the story for me. When I got home, what did I find at my doorstep? A demon. For me, I saw the demon in my spirit right there at the door, and he looked like the grim reaper. He was a spirit of death and proceeded to torment me that night with terrible thoughts. The Lord soon told me that I couldn't cast the spirit out of the little boy because I was in agreement with that spirit. Of course, that was a shocking thing to be told from the Lord.

It was a major wake-up call. The Lord had been trying to tell me that for months, but I wasn't really listening. In this moment, however, I was. He told me the reason I couldn't resurrect that boy was because I loved my violent guy movies and video games. You know, the ones that had revenge as the motivator for the movie theme or the game. There was something inside of me that had to see the bad guys killed. You could feel it. I just didn't realize it till the Lord named it as the spirit of death and told me I was basically partnering with it by enjoying those forms of entertainment.

GAINING AUTHORITY BY FASTING EVIL

I spent the next few months fasting from all forms of death and revengeful movies. The lesson was driven home by the Lord. I got the point. This was serious business. If I was to have authority over the devil, I couldn't be operating in the same realm he operates in. I couldn't enjoy seeing people get revenge, bad guys getting killed and justice looking like death before I could be satisfied.

I'm so thankful for the mercy of God. He wants us to be victorious over the devil, but sometimes we don't realize that we are sleeping with the enemy. It's Samson and Delijah. He thought he could continually sleep with the enemy without it costing him something. It ended up costing him his life. Proverbs 7 says that if you sleep with the immoral woman, she will take you all the way to the grave (verses 24-27):

> *"Now then, my sons, listen to me; pay attention to what I say. Do not let your heart turn to her ways or stray into her paths. Many are the victims she has brought down; her slain are a mighty throng. Her house is a highway to the grave, leading down to the chambers of death."*

We have to recognize we are in a war. We can't be dancing with the devil and then want to have authority over the devil when the demons come for payment. I've seen too many people feel invincible in a moment of prayer, but then destroyed later on because they had a secret issue in their life they didn't want to get free of.

I remember one guy from my church who started living with a lady; a lady who was not his wife. He tried to convince me that God was pleased with him because he could still speak in tongues. I told him he was missing the whole point and indeed God was not happy with him. He was destroying himself and his whole family in doing this.

Just as the sons of Sceva couldn't cast out the demon that left them naked, neither can we cast out something, no matter how loudly we shout at it, if we are in agreement with it. Spiritual warfare is a great way to get free of whatever bondage is inside of us. As I've mentioned, I know that when I go somewhere, that area is going to test me. It is going to give me an opportunity to encounter God in a new way. Sometimes I go to a location and I just get lots of revelation. I am so thankful for the city types where the heavens are easily opened in those cities. Then there are other times when I go somewhere, and I get mentally beat up.

A couple years ago, I went to another state to do a conference for the first time in that area. They were excited to host me at someone's cabin that overlooked the mountains. The cabin itself was nice enough, but when I entered the bedroom, it was dark in the spirit. There were some African relics in there from the cabin owner's childhood journey as a missionary kid.

One of those relics was definitely packing some demonic funk on it. I tried to sleep, yet all I felt was absolute darkness. I wrestled and saw all sorts of funky, unrestful things. I tried to bind the enemy and nothing happened.

Early in the morning after a sleepless night, knowing I was to preach all day, I heard the Lord say go sleep on the living room coach. It's amazing that he cares about those things. After a few more minutes of trying to sleep on the bed I responded. The living room couch wasn't as comfortable as the bed, but just leaving the room allowed me to sleep. Whatever atmosphere was in that other room wasn't strong enough to follow me a few feet away into the living room. I'm thankful for that.

UNDERSTANDING AUTHORITY

Sometimes demonic activity only has a very limited reach. Like for me, just leaving that room brought peace. Other times, a demonic atmosphere can be over a city, a region or a person. Sometimes I go to a particular fast food restaurant. Every time I go into that place at one location, I'll feel lust. There is another restaurant exactly like that in another part of town. When I go to that location instead, I feel great. I've learned that the owners of that one location have allowed activity, knowingly or unknowingly, that has happened in that place that can affect everyone who enters. Do I have authority to bind and loose there? Not unless I have been given permission. It doesn't mean that spirit is going to hurt me, it just means I'll probably sense that spirit when I'm there. I'll taste of its thoughts and emotions, and it may not be very fun to be there unless I can turn off the sense of that evil presence.

I remember staying at someone else's guest house when I was preaching at a certain church. My son and I both were staying at the same house. We had the place all to ourselves. The house itself was very nice and clean, but the room my son was sleeping in was all the way across the house. He didn't really want to sleep by himself in a new house, so I told him he could sleep in my bed with me. That was a grand idea, other than my son was tossing and turning that night and I couldn't sleep. I was glad he was sleeping, but I decided to quietly go to the other room where he was before he joined me.

As soon as I got in that room, I was clobbered by all sorts of evil thoughts. I couldn't sleep a lick that night. The next day I was to preach, so I went to the pastor and told him what was going on in that guesthouse. At first, he was perplexed. But after investigating, he came back and told me they had a group of ladies staying at that house when no one else was there. The one lady using the room I was in had some terrible bondages in her life she was trying to come out of agreement with.

Oh, the joys for me. I had to feel all that junk. I had the pastor come over that night and told him to please take authority over that spirit. My son and I were both praying with him, and both of us started to retch at the same time. Retching is what I call spiritually cleaning something out. It's not retching where you physically throw up, but at some levels it feels the same. In that moment, we started to retch a little. It is a way of getting rid of some spiritual funk that has tried to get on you or on someone.

Sometimes I can get rid of the demonic that way in a room or house, and at other times I can't. There may be a reason why you can't get rid of something. That is why Jesus would ask someone who had a sickness, etc., "Do you want to be healed?" He needed the power of agreement to get things done. Even Jesus himself couldn't just barge right in and cast out every devil. The one boy who had a demon the disciples couldn't get rid of needed a father who believed. The father confessed he believed and asked the Lord to help his unbelief. That was enough for Jesus to be able to swoop in and take out the demon. Read what Mark 9:23-25 says:

> "'If you can?' said Jesus. 'Everything is possible for one who believes.'
>
> Immediately the boy's father exclaimed, 'I do believe; help me overcome my unbelief!' When Jesus saw that a crowd was running to the scene, he rebuked the impure spirit. 'You deaf and mute spirit,' he said, 'I command you, come out of him and never enter him again.'"

GETTING AGREEMENT

Sometimes we need the agreement of whoever's house, business, church, etc., we are at to take authority over whatever is going on there. The same goes with a person. There have been times when I could have easily gotten someone free of a demon living in them, but they weren't ready to get free. It has been in those moments when I've had to allow that person to stay under the bondage of the demon until they are ready to be free. It's sad to watch, but people have authority in their own lives.

Sometimes I'm in a situation where I feel something, and I am supposed to do something about it. Sometimes I feel something, but I'm not supposed to do anything about it. Other times I have to learn to turn my feeler off.

This has taken me a long time to learn. I always felt that if I didn't feel the bad and the ugly in a room, city, church or region, I was grieving God. I didn't realize that the gift God gave me of discernment of spirits, through my feeler, was a gift and not something I *had to* use all the time.

It is easier to understand this if you think about another gift of the spirit: the gift of healing. Is it my job to pray for every sick person that I see? Should I stop every person in a wheelchair to pray for their healing? There may be seasons when I should do that, but in other seasons I've had to learn that caring for my family and not stopping to pray for every need I see is actually a key to healthy, long-term family. I need to just turn off my sensors that are looking for people to pray for healing.

TURN YOUR FEELER OFF

In the same way, I have the choice to not turn my feeler on concerning what is going on in every single room I enter. I've had to learn this the hard way. Sometimes I'll come home from a big, anointed meeting that I either was leading or apart of. My spirit man is really dialed up in those times. In moments like that, I choose not to watch TV. The moment I turn TV on, I can tell I'm at another level of sensitivity and way more susceptible to whatever unhealthy, soulish, fear-based or perverse things are going on there. At other times, I may have a grace to watch something that's not overtly evil but has a few funky vibes in it. But when my spirit is dialed up, I have to protect my spirit.

Another example is when I'll go into a room and feel the funk and decide right then and there to turn my feeler off. You may be wondering, "Is that okay? Can I do that?" Turning your feeler off is not the same thing as grieving the spirit of God. This is ruling your gift.

I used to go into restaurants and would be so picky with the waiter/
waitress about where I should sit. I'd scan the place and think, "I don't want
to sit over there…some funky people are over there." I'd then ask them
to please sit me over somewhere where there seemed to be no drama or
strangeness going on in conversation, etc. But more often than not, some
other person would come in and sit at the table near mine anyway, and they
would be funky in their spirit or actions. I learned that I could either be
paying such close attention to what everyone was thinking and feeling or
just enjoy myself.

Enjoying myself and the ones I was with was an intentional choice I
had to make. I'd go into a movie theater and decide to sit and watch the
movie and not focus on anybody who might sit next to me. I started getting
breakthrough when I could go and enjoy my family at the movies and not
even notice who was sitting next to me. I didn't care who they were. I wasn't
going to feel their spiritual climate and decide if they were safe to sit next
to or not. I was just going to trust God is good, that I am okay and I am not
going to be hurt by someone sitting next to me.

You see, sometimes I can shift someone's environment, and other times
I'm supposed to shift my own. I'm not always responsible to bind every
spirit I come across. I need to know what my assignment is.

Sometimes I get around people who think that wherever they go they
are called to take out the devil nearby. When I hear their intentions, I think
to myself, "I'm not sure that is the best way to do things." Sometimes we
need to know what our assignment is. That helps us determine what fights
we should be in (and which ones we shouldn't). Maybe the reason we are
not able to get rid of some spirit that is attacking us is because we don't have
an authority to deal with that particular spirit.

One time I came back from Washington DC after ten days there with
my family doing ministry and sight-seeing. The whole time we were there I

YOU CAN'T CAST OUT DEVILS...

had been clobbered in the spirit. I was thinking about how challenging that trip was when the Lord spoke. He spoke 15 minutes before we landed back in California on my flight home.

He said. "You went there on your own."

"What?" I thought.

I thought I had been sent there. You see, I had been blessed by my local leaders to travel, and that was also my income stream in that season. The Lord showed me when he spoke that I went on my own. My heart had the attitude that no one else cared about me. Traveling was something I had to fight for, and no one would give me an easy handout. Therefore, I went on my own. He showed me I needed to learn to pull those who actually had already sent me out into my heart.

DON'T GO ALONE

Here's what I mean: I started a strategy that whenever I went somewhere, I would say, "I am not being sent on my own. I am being sent with the blessing of..." and then I would name whichever spiritual fathers or mothers I was in relationship with who knew what I was doing and who were blessing me. That created a protection and authority on the assignment I was in. Sometimes we can't cast out a devil and end the warfare around us because we are not in the right heart posture in that place.

Think about the unnecessary warfare you may be going through just because you don't have authority to get rid of that warfare. In your heart you are not having the right attitude, therefore you are not covered. I'm sure you've heard this question: "Who is your covering?" My definition of covering does include spiritual leaders, etc., who I am in relationship with, but I also like to say when asked that question, that love covers. I picked that up from one of my spiritual fathers, Wendell McGowen.

I've learned that love is a great covering of protection and gives us authority over the enemy. When you don't have love for somewhere or someone, then you don't have authority to deal with their demons or be free of the spiritual warfare that is there. Love is a protection. I often pray out loud when I go somewhere about how I am not on my own, proclaiming whose authority I am under. I also spend time praying for the place I'm going to until I feel love oozing out of my heart and prayers flow freely for those people. If I get love, I get covered. If I get covered, then I am under authority.

When I am under authority, I have authority to declare things in the spiritual realm. I can boot out the devil and bring in the angelic and Kingdom agenda through my declarations. The centurion understood this principle when he told Jesus to just say the word and his servant would be healed. He then went on and talked about the authority structure he was a part of and how the Kingdom was the same. Jesus commended the guy for his faith, and then spoke a word that did indeed heal his servant. Here it is in Matthew 8:8-10:

> *"The centurion replied, 'Lord, I do not deserve to have you come under my roof. But just say the word, and my servant will be healed. For I myself am a man under authority, with soldiers under me. I tell this one, 'Go,' and he goes; and that one, 'Come,' and he comes. I say to my servant, 'Do this,' and he does it.' When Jesus heard this, he was amazed and said to those following him, 'Truly I tell you, I have not found anyone in Israel with such great faith.'"*

You see, when you are under authority, you have authority to speak words of healing, to bind the works of the enemy, and to bring God's Kingdom to earth through your submitted heart.

USE WISDOM

We need to learn to be wise as serpents and innocent as doves. Sometimes we are zealously fighting battles that we don't have authority to be in on or even have a strategy for. Joshua had one win under his belt, and then the people of Israel got defeated because they didn't submit to the Lord and find out his strategy. Joshua 8:10-12 tells the story:

> *"The Lord said to Joshua, 'Stand up! What are you doing down on your face? Israel has sinned; they have violated my covenant, which I commanded them to keep. They have taken some of the devoted things; they have stolen, they have lied, they have put them with their own possessions. That is why the Israelites cannot stand against their enemies; they turn their backs and run because they have been made liable to destruction. I will not be with you anymore unless you destroy whatever among you is devoted to destruction.'"*

In Joshua 9:14, they had another situation where they got deceived because they didn't ask the Lord what he thought.

> *"The Israelites sampled their provisions but did not inquire of the Lord."*

One of the ways we lose battles with the enemy is when we are not submitted to God and asking about his strategies. Why was David a man after God's own heart? It was because he inquired of the Lord often and concerning everything he did, including the battles he would engage. 1 Samuel 23:4 says, "Once again David inquired of the Lord..."

In those situations, God would meet David and tell him to either fight, or to get out of there because he'd be defeated or handed over to the enemy.

We need to learn to ask God and not assume we know what is going on just because we have some wisdom or experience. Protection comes at times from God's wisdom, not from our might nor our power.

Sometimes we can be like Moses who used his might and power to cause water to come out of the rock, but we miss getting to go into the fullness of God's promises. It's because we don't wait for the Spirit of the Lord's directives. Read about Moses in Numbers 20:11-12:

> *"Then Moses raised his arm and struck the rock twice with his staff. Water gushed out, and the community and their livestock drank. But the Lord said to Moses and Aaron, 'Because you did not trust in me enough to honor me as holy in the sight of the Israelites, you will not bring this community into the land I give them.'"*

That's a great example of someone using their gifting, but notice the difference between using his gifting from a place of frustration vs. doing what God said to do, "Speak to the rock." When we are using principles instead of Holy Spirit-initiated fresh strategies and we go to binding and loosing spiritual things, we find ourselves like Moses, outside of the fullness of what could have been ours.

Understand that walking in the things of the Spirit needs to be God initiated, not just a passion of ours for God. This is a key distinction between walking in victory and getting defeated. I want us to learn where our authority is and when we need God's strategy, but I also want us to learn to avoid the pitfalls of presumptuous behaviors that end up causing casualties in our lives or the lives of the people around us.

CHAPTER EIGHT

SELF-INFLICTED WARFARE

———

I am a warrior as I've said before. My name means "Meant for Battle." My lovely wife has told me at times that I need another identity as well, not just *warrior*. She reminds me that I shouldn't always be on the lookout for a fight. I agree. I've learned and probably will always be learning the balance of being a warrior and enjoying the journey. The warrior identity is about taking territory, but part of being able to go the long-haul is knowing when to fight and when to rest.

Elijah was quite a warrior. He had to be. An evil queen and a bad king ruled the land of Israel; the land that belonged to God. There were many prophets being killed, and the people of God were truly in need of reviving. This was a legitimate battle for a prophet. Elijah was up for the task.

It is not a question of *if* we fight when God tells us to, but when we fight, how we fight and with whom we fight. Elijah had a God-given assignment to restore the people of Israel back to God. In my opinion, the way he fought needed a little bit of wisdom.

If you have been in the church a while, you should know this story well. Elijah called for a confrontation with the forces of evil and the forces of good. It was Elijah against the prophets of Baal and the prophets of Asherah. As they built their altar to call on their false god to send fire down, Elijah used the battle tactic of sarcasm and jesting. After he was done making fun of the prophets of Baal, he then built his altar and prayed. Of course, we know the story and know God answered by fire. That's amazing. I want to make a side note here that just because we see the power of God displayed, it doesn't mean God is pleased or we have done everything correctly in how we are handling the spirit realm.

Take for example Moses who used his rod to strike the rock and water indeed did come out. What a miracle, right? Not in God's sight. Water came out, but Moses was kept out of the Promised Land because he used spiritual gifts with the wrong fruit from the wrong spirit: anger. The same went for Elijah. He used sarcasm and jesting when coming at the enemy.

HOW SHOULD I FIGHT?

I've seen prophets, vocational ministers, and saints in the moment of the glory and in the heat of the battle begin to make some mighty declarations against the enemy. They bind this and that spirit. They call the devil all sorts of foul names. "The devil is stupid, a dummy and I'm here to crush him!" they say. Or something of that nature.

I've heard other developing or immature prophets speak unwise things when the anointing is there or when the crowd is really revved up from worship or because of the desire to hear the developing prophet. I'll hear the prophet talk about how easily they've dealt with the devil in the past. I'll hear them share their war stories like they are the invincible superhero. The problem is I know some of them. I know they are struggling in real life and that the enemy is winning over them more than they are winning over the devil. In front of people they seem so large and powerful, but when they are alone, they are like Elijah when he is alone.

Let's go back to that. Elijah has his moment of victory, then he had another. He went to the top of the mountain and he started to pray for rain. Rain did come after he prayed seven times. God loved Elijah. But what happened later on? He heard a word from Jezebel saying she was going to kill him. It sent him running. He wanted to end his life. Here's the story in 1 Kings 19:1-3:

> *"Now Ahab told Jezebel everything Elijah had done and how he had killed all the prophets with the sword. So Jezebel sent a messenger to Elijah to say, 'May the gods deal with me, be it ever so severely, if by this time tomorrow I do not make your life like that of one of them.' Elijah was afraid and ran for his life."*

How in the world did this happen? I believe it came through the door of sarcasm and unauthorized taunting. Jude 1:8-10 tells us where the open door was for the enemy to take out Elijah.

> *"In the very same way, these dreamers pollute their own bodies, reject authority and slander celestial beings. But even the archangel Michael, when he was disputing with the devil about the body of Moses did not dare to bring a slanderous accusation against him, but said, 'The Lord rebuke you!' Yet these men speak abusively against whatever they do not understand; and what things they do not understand by instinct, like unreasoning animals- these are the very things that destroy them."*

When you are in the anointing or in the heat of the battle you can feel invincible. Elijah felt unshakable in that moment. He not only saw fire come down, but rain too. The problem is whatever goes up must come down, and he crashed hard when he fell. Sometimes we crash really hard because we betrayed the principles of Jude. We started to slander the devil in the moment of the anointing or in the heat of the battle. There is definitely a time to deal with the devil, to cast him out, to bind him, to take authority over him, and to evict him. It's not always about just getting him out of your territory or situation, but it's about the *way* you evict him.

I know this from years of experience: when I am feeling the highs of the anointing, I cannot allow that moment to deceive me into thinking I'm a rock star. Neither do I let that moment cause me to start making brash declarations at the devil.

This lesson hit home years ago when I went to the Brazilian statue of Jesus that stands tall over Rio De Janeiro. I had never been there before, so when we got there, we noticed a shrine to an idol at the base of the Jesus statue. The idol supposedly was pulled out of the water and was sacred. People were giving money to it, and it also had lots of candles lit around it. The spirit of heaviness was so strong in that area, the strongest I'd ever felt anywhere until then. In that moment, along with a few other intercessors, I began to bind that spirit and command it to leave.

For weeks following that event I had a lot of spiritual backlash come against me. I was up there making fun of that spirit and commanding it to go. It wasn't until later when God showed me how that opened up the door of the enemy to come at me. He spoke to me about it and reminded me of a situation when I was on another prayer walk, when I was starting to feel high and mighty in a moment when the Spirit was evident and present. When my words started rising and I started sarcastically going after the enemy, the Lord reminded me of that verse in Jude. All of a sudden, the fear of the Lord came upon me. I realized the unnecessary warfare backlash I had received numerous times was because I wasn't operating in wisdom in dealing with the enemy.

WHAT DOES WISDOM SAY?

We know that taking territory for God is invigorating. There is a powerful feeling you get to experience when the anointing is on you and you are provoked to deal with some enemy that might be in your midst. The wisdom in those moments is to not assume you know all there is to know about what's going on. Every moment needs to be God initiated. Allow him to lead you and recognize the power you are experiencing is not going to last. It will be there for that moment, but when the moment passes, you will be normal again.

Elijah returned to his normal state when he was done with his prophetic acts. Since Elijah was a loner already, he returned to his loner state when done. He began to complain to the Lord that he was the only one; the only one left with zeal for the Lord. You see, the enemy hit him where he was vulnerable. Jezebel said, "I'm going to get you, Elijah." Here is her threat recorded in 1 Kings 19:2,

> *"May the gods deal with me, be it ever so severely, if by this time tomorrow I do not make your life like that of one of them."*

The unclean spirit hit the place in him that said he was all alone, unprotected, vulnerable. The truth of the matter was that he was doing just fine. God had been with him for a long time, and he had always been protected. He also wasn't the only one left serving God, because Obadiah had just told him he had kept hidden 100 other prophets. There was Obadiah, another 100 prophets and then God told him there were actually 7000 more who hadn't bowed their knees to Baal. Obadiah, in 1 Kings 18:13, says,

> *"Haven't you heard, my lord, what I did while Jezebel was killing the prophets of the Lord? I hid a hundred of the Lord's prophets in two caves, fifty in each, and supplied them with food and water."*

And God speaks to Elijah in 1 Kings 19:18,

"Yet I reserve seven thousand in Israel—all whose knees have not bowed down to Baal and whose mouths have not kissed him."

Battle reveals areas of vulnerability in us that need God's healing. That is why when I am in battle, I want to keep the cloak of humility on. When the battle ends, my weaknesses may be exploited if I am not wise.

Recently we hosted our first Emerging Prophets conference. In some ways it was a battle, and at the same time a great victory too. There were some very high prophetic moments, and God did a lot during that conference. It was also something we had built up to for several months, and so the accomplishment was fulfilling.

Right after the conference, my wife went off to Mexico for a couple days on a mission trip. I knew her trip was coming up and knew I would be mostly alone after the high of the conference. I know the Elijah place well, as I've experienced a few of the highs and lows and could relate to his victories and struggles.

FORESEEING THE CHALLENGES

I foresaw potential challenges with loneliness, knowing Heather would be gone. Loneliness can lead to a lot of other things, such as unrealistic fears, impurity, etc. I planned times with my parents, my son and friends during the time when Heather was gone to make sure that after the battle, I would remain intact. Did I want to be alone? On one hand yes, just to recover after giving out so much in the previous months all the way up to the conference. But I knew I needed people more in that moment than aloneness.

You see, it's important to understand our weaknesses and what happens to us before, during and after battles, whatever the battle may be. I have learned that to be a healthy prophet who goes the distance (or a healthy saint for that matter), you learn to remain at a consistent pace in the journey. Learning to treat Christianity like an enjoyable marathon is a healthier mindset than doing numerous sprints.

Sprinting Christians are the type who start out great, but don't get very far. Several decades ago, I overheard Bill Johnson say to come back after 20 years and tell him you're still burning for God, and then he'd vouch that you were a revivalist (something along those lines). I got the point. The point was to learn to not be a fast start who doesn't finish the race. By the way…I'm still burning for Jesus 20 years after I first heard Bill say that.

Learning wisdom in warfare is strategic. Do you know yourself? Do you know your tendencies? Do you how you tend to react when you get into high, tense situations? Do you tend to curse people when you don't do well? Do you tend to get angry and irrational? Do you tend to go silent and become a loner when you are going through difficult things? Do you tend to start getting protective and pulling away from everyone in the thick of a tense situation? Do you tend to want to lash out at people and become rude with your words when you are irritated or tired? Understanding yourself is a part of being able to navigate battles well.

We don't want to be the kind of people who are taken out by the enemy in an area we could have avoided. Sometimes in my world of training prophets, I see tendencies with certain prophet types. Loneliness is definitely one of those tendencies. It's important for prophetic folks or others to recognize where their weakness is and to work at pressing into relationships. Sometimes it takes a while to get relationships to really work for you. That is a good, worthwhile battle to fight.

Don't just focus on the battle of your church, region or nation. Focus on the battle you are fighting that keeps you from believing people would want to hang out with you. If you can't defeat that battle, then when you get into the battle against the enemy over your region or another nation, you will find the devil waiting for the perfect time to find a legal right to take you out of commission. He can do that when you have not honored the biblical principle of staying connected to the body of Christ at a deep level. Isolation is a killer.

The devil will wait till you feel like you are really winning in some area, and then he will hit the button of distrust. You may be rising up to succeed in some business venture, but you don't really trust anyone. At the moment the business seems to be getting breakthrough, he will cause there to be a mistrust in your heart. He will poke that button until you sabotage a key relationship, and your business venture will come crashing down.

All of that can be avoided if you keep yourself in humility and work at staying connected to the body of Christ. You don't have to be perfect to make it victoriously; you just need to be healthily connected to God and people. Sometimes our most powerful weapon in warfare is not something we can do, but it is something God did.

CHAPTER NINE

AN ENEMY WITH NO MOUTH, FEET OR ARMS

[rpm Ministries] > "Soul Physicians"
By: Robert W. Kellemen

I used to preach that the devil has been defeated and disarmed, but he has a big mouth. He is always accusing us. One day the Lord stopped me in the middle of saying that and said, "Keith, you cut off the feet and the hands of the devil, but I also closed his mouth."

Colossians 1:22-23 confirms what the Lord said:

NIV

"But now he has reconciled you by Christ's physical body through death to present you holy in his sight, without blemish and free from accusation – if you continue in your faith, established and firm, and do not move from the hope held out in the gospel."

In this passage, it shows we are free of the accuser and the words that come out of his mouth. Sometimes we allow unnecessary warfare because we believe that the warfare is allowed. We allow warfare through wrong theologies like the one I just shared. I grew up in a culture that advocated Revelations 12 – the passage that talks about the devil being in the heavens,

wrong teaching

but eventually being hurled down. The famous part of that passage is found in verses 11-12:

> "For the accuser of our brothers and sisters, who accuses them before our God day and night has been hurled down. They triumphed over him by the blood of the lamb and by the word of their testimony; they did not love their lives so much as to shrink from death."

The context in which people shared that passage was that the devil is in your heavens, but you can overcome him one day through Jesus' blood, your testimony and daily being willing to lay your life down for God.

YOU ARE FREE FROM ACCUSATION

It sounds good, but it gave the devil the power to accuse because he is still in your heavens. Colossians 1 is a better way to look at the devil. You are free from accusation. He is not in your heavens; he is already cast down by what Jesus did.

The other parts of our victory over the devil were parts I had already discovered; parts where the devil had lost his feet and arms. Colossians 2:15 talks about the disarming part:

> "And *having* disarmed the powers and authorities, he made a public spectacle of them, triumphing over them by the cross."

The devil has no arms. His power to destroy you has been taken away. He's also lost his feet, and most importantly he's lost his voice into your life. That's what it means when God has shut his mouth. You are free of the accuser saying you are not enough, you can't do it, you will be defeated, you are disqualified, or you cannot succeed. If you want to win in warfare, you have got to learn to shut down his voice. Colossians 1:22-23 has become one of my biggest victories against the enemy in this season. It has helped me in so many valuable ways.

When the enemy comes at me to disqualify me, accusing me of having sin in my life, I fall back into Colossians 1: I am blameless. The enemy tries to get us to agree with sin by accusing us that we are sinful. But I know I am blameless. He can't accuse me of being worthy of blame. He can't accuse me of being an evil sinner. Why? Because I am blameless. That means without blame.

When I begin to own that I am not worthy of being blamed, then I'll stop inviting the devil's blame and accusation. He is always accusing, but I don't have to listen to it. The devil will try to tell you you're dirty, and he's caught you in some thought that isn't of God. In that moment, you have to be able to say, "Devil, I am blameless, and I am free of accusation."

How am I able to sustain being free of accusation? Colossians 1:23 shows how..."If you continue in the faith..." What is the faith you are to continue in? Ephesians 2:8-9 answers that question:

> *"For it is by grace you have been saved, through faith—and this is not from yourselves, it is the gift of God—not by works, so that no one can boast."*

So, what is the faith? It is the gift of God. How are you free from being defeated? Because you continue in the faith: faith in God and the faith of God.

During warfare, the enemy likes to come at us and hurl thoughts at us from afar – hopeless thoughts, lustful thoughts, fearful thoughts, etc. He'll then lob a thought of shame and guilt at us next. He'll say, "How could you call yourself a Christian and have that lustful thought? You're so bad!" You have to counter him with, "I am blameless and free of accusation, and devil, those thoughts are yours not mine. I'm a person after God's own heart!"

Remind yourself that "There is no more condemnation for those who are in Christ Jesus" (Romans 12:1). You are in Christ Jesus, right? Yes, you are. Galatians 2:20 says,

> *"I have been crucified with Christ and I no longer live..."*

When the devil comes to lodge an illegal accusation against you, he'll say, "You're guilty." You get to say right back, "I am not alive anymore. I've been crucified, and Christ lives within." When the devil comes at you, you overcome him by reminding yourself of why you are blameless and free of accusation. You are blameless because the one inside of you doesn't sin. You are free of accusation because the accuser's mouth has been completely shut down by Jesus' finished work at the cross.

"DON'T OWN THE ENEMIES THOUGHTS"

The enemy tries to get you to own the thoughts he throws at you. If he can get you to own them, he has you. My Grandpa Lewallen used to tell me that I needed to first of all, *not* repent for the thoughts the enemy threw at me, because repentance was ownership. Now, if I give in to the thoughts and start entertaining them, then I should repent of them. But just because I have a temptation doesn't mean I have given into the temptation. He's the tempter. Not me. I am pure. I am made in God's image. I am prone to do right.

You see, knowing the finished work of Jesus is so critical for us to be able to victoriously combat the devil. Part of the finished work of Jesus is found in the understanding of the armor of God. I grew up putting on the full armor of God in Ephesians 6. The shield of faith, the sword of the spirit, the helmet of salvation, etc. It was a good exercise and a good time to hide the Word in my heart. But really learning what each one of those weapons are is critical if you are to be victorious. Just reciting them daily and declaring you have put on the full armor of God is not the same thing as having revelation of what every one of the armor pieces are, and then being intentional about using them.

Let's take a minute to go through each one of them. Ephesians 6:13-17 says,

> *"Therefore put on the full armor of God, so that when the day of evil comes, you may be able to stand your ground, and after you have done everything, to stand. Stand firm then, with the belt of truth buckled around your waist, with the breastplate of righteousness in place, and with your feet fitted with the readiness that comes from the gospel of peace. In addition to all this, take up the shield of faith, with which you can extinguish all the flaming arrows of the evil one. Take the helmet of salvation and the sword of the Spirit, which is the word of God."*

The first piece of our armor is the belt of truth. What is the belt of truth that we have to stand firm with? To me, the belt of truth is all about vulnerability. You have to stand firm in the fact that vulnerability is truth. Truth means in the light and nothing hidden. So, to have the belt of truth around your waist, you have committed to being real in the deepest parts of who you are.

The armor is a practical way that Paul breaks down different characteristics of God. Only God gives us the victory over the devil. God has no darkness in him; he is fully light. Even when on earth the devil came to Jesus, and Scripture said he could find nothing in him. John 14:30 in the NKJV says,

"...the ruler of this world is coming, and he has nothing in Me."

(* In the light / Real / Nothing hidden)

NOTHING HIDDEN

There was nothing hidden inside Jesus. Everything was in the light. One of the ways we get authority in spiritual warfare and an ability to be victorious is to learn to live in the light. Find mentors who you can be vulnerable with. Find friends, and if you're married your spouse as well, who you can share everything with. Who can hear the good, bad and ugly of your life? Is everything about your life known? That is what the belt of truth is all about.

I've learned, through years of fighting for this, who to be vulnerable with and with what parts of me. Certain people can only handle certain parts of my life. I have to know who can handle what area of my life. For more insights on this, read my book, *Reforming the Church from a House to a Home.*

The second part of the armor is the breastplate of righteousness. I like to say the breastplate is his acceptance that covers our heart. It's what he did – his righteousness.

What covers my heart and keeps me living from acceptance instead of from rejection or out of performance? It's knowing what he did at the cross accomplished all the work that was needed in my life. My righteousness is as filthy rags, but his righteousness is what I learn to live from. If I truly am living under his righteousness, then when I don't have a perfect day, don't say all the right things or think all the right things, I still can live in the delight of the Father over me. I'm well pleasing to him and he is happy with me. That is living under his righteousness.

This piece of armor is so critical, because as we try to do great things for God, the devil will come along and try to make us feel guilty. He'll try to get us to feel we are not good enough or not enough for the task. It is in those moments we have to remind ourselves that God's righteousness covers us and we are accepted because of what he did, not because of what we do or don't do.

#3

Next, you need to have your feet fitted with the Gospel of peace. Peace crushes Satan. Peace is an amazing, New Covenant weapon. Peace can be relational harmony. Peace can be internal rest in your thoughts. Peace can also be the ability to rest in God's goodness in the middle of the storm. It's seen in Jesus' ability to rest when the disciples were freaking out. Here's an example in Matthew 8:24:

> *"Suddenly a furious storm came up on the lake, so that the waves swept over the boat. But Jesus was sleeping."*

Peace gave him the authority to crush Satan and calm the storm. This peace is what we carry with us wherever we go. It's what you have your feet fitted with. Wherever you go, you bring your peace. When you enter a house, you are to put your peace on that house. If they don't receive it, you never lose your peace. You just internalize it and keep the peace.

PEACE CRUSHES FEAR

Peace crushes fear. I remember when I went into a New Age store and felt the funky atmosphere of some of the statues. I was starting to get anxious, and the Lord told me to hold my peace. You see, peace is a weapon. If you lose peace, you've lost. Peace is only sustained when I trust. I have to trust that someone bigger than me is in charge and is with me and is watching over me. I'm not just trusting trust; I'm trusting a good Father who sent Jesus to live inside me. The one who lives inside of me is trustworthy.

#4 Then there is the shield of faith. Oh, I love the faith shield! It's by grace you have been saved, through faith, and this is not of yourself. I love the revelation of faith. Faith is not ours. It's not of ourselves; it's his. Faith is connected to someone. Have faith in God. So, the shield of faith is the revelation that God is our protection. Putting on the shield is the confidence that he is watching out for me and the knowledge that he is a good Father who will never leave me nor forsake me. I can trust that my shield of faith, which quenches all the fiery darts of the enemy, is actually God. God himself is my shield.

I am not my own shield. It's not my big declarations that do anything for me. I'm not the big man of faith. Some people like to think of themselves as a person of faith. They have great faith, yes. But I know that my faith is the faith of God. It's *his* faith; he gave it to me. This faith is what saved us, but it was not of ourselves; it was a gift of God.

God can extinguish all the fiery darts of the enemy. I love that. Our shield of faith is the reliance on God to protect every part of us. I don't have to wonder if I'm strong enough to protect myself against the works of the enemy, I just have to lean on the one who is strong enough.

Reading Psalm 91 is such a blessing when I need a reminder of his protection over me and all that pertains to me. As I read it, I find myself and situations I am wrestling with in that chapter. If I am afraid about my kids' protection, I am going to dig into the part of Psalm 91 where it talks about no harm will come near my tent. Here is Psalm 91:10-11:

> *"No harm will overtake you; no disaster will come near your tent.*
> *For he will command his angels concerning you to guard you in*
> *all your ways."*

I know my family is under my tent, and I am under his shadow. I am going to do whatever it takes to see him as my shield and make sure I rest in his promises. His shield totally annihilates every flaming arrow of the enemy. Every lie that comes against me to create fear, as long as I can see that lie for what it is and keep a mindset that sees his protection, then I am safe from all harm.

The enemy can, at times, create images in our head that something

horrible is happening to a loved one or is going to happen to us. It is in those
moments, I have to fall back on God's promise of protection in Scripture
and also in my prophetic words. I have one prophetic word that my family
is protected like the President of our country is protected. When fear tries
to grip me, I have to fall back into what God said and recognize he is with
me and cares about everyone I care about.

A HEALTHY MINDSET

The helmet of salvation is next. What is the helmet about? The helmet
of salvation is a mindset of health. Salvation means to be saved, healed,
delivered and whole. The mindset from Christ that covers my thoughts are
ones of health, wholeness, freedom and eternal life. My mind is not to be
filled with thoughts of doubt, insecurity, woundedness, brokenness, and
sin. My mind is whole. My thoughts are fixed above. My mind is set apart
for him. I am his and I have his thoughts. My thoughts are his thoughts, and
because of that, my ways are his ways. I have the mind of Christ. I don't have
my own mind; I have his mind. That is the only way I am able to overcome
the devil.

"Not by might, nor by power, but by his spirit says the Lord."
Zech. 4:6

I am not able to overcome the devil in my might but because I have
God's mind, I am an overcomer.

Finally, I am to take up the sword of the Spirit, which is the Word of
God. The Word of God is our offensive weapon. I am not able to kill the
enemy defensively but rather just keep him from taking over. But the Word
of God will knock Satan out. Even Jesus himself did not combat the devil
with his own words, but with the Word of God.

Jesus repeatedly said to the devil in Matthew 4, "It is written!" The devil would come and give a half truth, even use a scripture from the Bible such as, "Throw yourself off this temple and he will protect you." Jesus would then return with another verse, "Test not the Lord."

We have to fight the devil when he comes at us with many thoughts that say we are not going to succeed. He'll throw at us pictures of our past failures or show us falling into sin. We have to fight the devil's thoughts and say, "No! The word of the Lord says over me that I will go the distance and I am an overcomer." We need to look at role models in the Bible like Joseph in the book of Genesis and declare that we are like them when the enemy comes in this way. We can say in that moment, "I am pure and am going to succeed, and my family will be blessed in every way."

You see, first we have to take the Word and know it well, but secondly, use it strategically. We can't randomly use verses that have nothing to do with our circumstances. We have to know specific verses that can take out the lies coming against us.

I love all that God has given us for victory. 2 Peter 1:3 says,

> *"His divine power has given us everything we need for life and godliness."*

We are not on the losing side. We can't help but win as long as we are using the right New Covenant weapons. Those weapons are the weapons of Christ and his finished work. That is where our protection is. That is where our victory is. Along with these time-tested weapons, we need to also access other parts of Christ's finished work – powerful things such as the blood of the Lamb.

CHAPTER TEN

ACCESSING THE PROTECTION THAT IS OURS

———

Trying to be invincible and strong because you have an anointing is not always wise. Sometimes we think we can win battles because we have giftings. When the anointing is there, people can feel invincible, but the only thing that has stood the test of time is the protection Jesus offers.

If we are going to take territory, we had better understand where our protection is. The protection I want to talk about here is three-fold: the blood of Jesus, the angels, and wisdom.

The blood of Jesus is something many of us have heard talked about for a long time. Taking communion is a part of the blood of Jesus. Some of us grew up taking communion as a part of the traditions of the church, but for me though, some of communion's power and life had become stale and diminished. The religious ceremony of it had stolen my joy for the blood and the body.

A few years ago, the Lord began to stretch my perspective about the blood and communion. My desire to see the rich traditions of our faith restored to vibrancy finally started paying off. I had been on the path to get back everything Jesus paid for, and I wanted it to be real to me. In the midst of this discovery, I began to find out that taking communion must come from revelation. Anything that has lost personal revelation becomes religious in nature and loses its power.

The blood is a powerful weapon against the devil if you have a revelation of the blood. Communion is powerful if you know what it does against the enemy and why.

HEAVENLY PROTOCOL

As I've learned how to go into heavenly places over the years, I've learned that there is a protocol. I can't go before the throne of God on my own; I go in the power of the blood and name of Jesus. His finished work is what gives us victory over the devil. There are times when I feel a resistance in the spirit from the devil. During those moments, I must be sure I have gone through the protocol of heaven if I am to shut down the devil.

First, I need to make sure that the blood of Jesus is accessed. The blood is accessed by faith and through declarations that apply it to our hearts, families, and surroundings. I need to also make sure I have no known sin in my life or judgements against anyone in my heart. If I am free of those, then I can confidently go before the Father to get protection, and then ultimately retribution on the enemy.

I love the old hymn, "The Blood Will Never Lose Its Power." There are no new tricks under the sun to take out the devil. We have to use what is timeless and tested. The blood of Jesus is our victory. His blood gives us power over sickness, disease, attack, lack of protection, etc. In the Old Covenant, they put the blood of the lamb over their doorposts and were protected. We have to put the blood of Jesus over the doorposts of our hearts and our homes. We don't do it out of fear, but out of confidence that this is our victory.

Communion, as a part of the blood, reminds me of the victory Jesus had over the devil. Every time I partake of communion, I want to make sure there is a depth of understanding and revelation that I am taking it from. I love Colossians 1 as a place of revelation for the blood. Colossians 1:20 says,

> *"And through him to reconcile to himself all things, whether things on earth or things in heaven by making peace through his blood, shed on the cross."*

The blood of Jesus brings me into relationship with God. It brings all things into relationship with God. That is what reconciliation is. When I am in relationship with God, I am protected from the enemy. My heart is synced up to what God wants. I am protected.

Another part of the protection that goes along with my heart being synced up to God is wisdom. Sometimes when we are in battle, the battle over a territory, we need the blood of Jesus as a protection. Other times, we need wisdom as a protection. They are both from the same source: Jesus. Jesus is our wisdom. That's why we need to pray for a spirit of wisdom and revelation as Paul prayed in Ephesians 1:17, that wisdom will give us eyes to see:

> *"I keep asking that the God of our Lord Jesus Christ, the glorious Father, may give you the Spirit of wisdom and revelation, so that you may know him better."*

I remember talking to my friend and mentor before I was going to another country. I had some money with me to use for the team I was overseeing. It was a significant amount of money to travel with, and my friend felt a warning from the Lord that someone might try to steal it.

He told me I needed to diversify the money in several places and with several people. I got a bit afraid, but he said, "Keith, I am believing that the diversification of the money will actually cause the enemy's plans to fail." It was true. I'm not sure if there would have been an attempt to steal the money, but I followed his advice and the money was safe. The wisdom of God may have very well caused the protection.

WISDOM IS NEEDED

In warfare we need wisdom. If we want to fight the good fight we are called to fight, we need to recognize there is a proper way to fight. I have had some Peter tendencies in my lifetime. Peter, at times, thought brute force would protect Jesus, and he used his sword to chop off an ear. Jesus had to rebuke him, and I'm sure Peter learned a valuable lesson that day from that rebuke. Sometimes it isn't our brute strength that is going to cause us to win against the devil. Sometimes we can feel invincible with our spiritual gifts, but it is wisdom that will cause us to win.

David knew about wisdom. Wisdom was found by David when he inquired of the Lord. He inquired of the Lord when the enemy first came at him after he was declared King. He had to fight the enemy twice. The first time, the Lord told him he could directly attack the enemy. The second time, he had to circle around from behind. See this in 2 Samuel 5:19:

> "So David inquired of the Lord, 'Shall I go and attack the Philistines? Will you deliver them into my hands?' The Lord answered him, 'Go, for I will surely deliver the Philistines into your hands.'"

Again, in 2 Samuel 5:23:

> "So David inquired of the Lord, and he answered, 'Do not go

straight up, but circle around behind them and attack them in
front of the poplar trees.'"

Wisdom helps us know how to fight. Fighting victoriously isn't about just fighting. It's not about the sheer willpower and strength of fighting, but it's about the wisdom of how to fight. Scripture says, "The horse is made ready for the day of battle, but victory rests with the Lord" (Proverbs 21:31). He has unique ways for us to win.

Sometimes we think that just by the sheer strength of yelling out binding and loosing prayers we will win against the enemy. Sometimes we feel we can defeat the devil by how loud and long we pray. No, it's by the wisdom of God that we will win against the enemy, and without that unique wisdom, we will be susceptible to defeat. That's the lesson we talked about previously with Joshua and Achan in Jericho.

We also see that David waited for the wisdom of God, and then got God's strategy. When he heard the sound of rustling in the trees, it would be time to fight. 2 Samuel 5:24 says,

"As soon as you hear the sound of marching in the tops of the
poplar trees, move quickly, because that will mean the Lord has
gone out in front of you to strike the Philistine army."

That sound was caused by angels. There is protection when we learn how to partner with the angels. Angels are another form of protection for us as believers.

PROTECTED BY ANGELS

I am convinced I've been protected many times by angels. I've had cars completely totaled in wrecks that I've been a part of, and I walked out of those cars with minor to no scratches. At other times, I have felt angels all around me, keeping me protected in hotel rooms I've stayed at where the area wasn't safe. Often times I've seen angels posted at the door.

Even though Lot, Abraham's nephew, was a bit dull to respond and wasn't paying attention to the fact that the city he lived in was completely corrupted, he was still protected by angels. He and his family were helped out of the city before it caught on fire and was completely destroyed. The Lord is so good and sends his angels to watch over us. Lot's story is in Genesis 19:16:

> "When he hesitated, the men grasped his hand and the hands of his wife and of his two daughters and led them safely out of the city, for the Lord was merciful to them."

I have had times when an angel of the Lord came in with a warning that humility was needed. The word the angel brought caused the fear of the Lord to come in and the ability to pay better attention to God's commands. If God's commands were not adhered to, there would have been consequences or even loss of protection.

I'm also very thankful for the times when I've been protected because an intercessor, even family members such as my parents or grandparents, prayed and God showed them something for me to watch out for. One time, my grandma called me and asked me if I was doing okay. She had a dream that I was being tempted, and it was accurate. The dream caused me to heed the fear of the Lord, respond, and in doing so find protection from temptation's harm.

There are many ways God protects us. The main thing is that we are paying attention to his protection and are appropriating it. Considering the battles we are in, protection is a part of the ability to go the distance as victorious warriors.

When my family and I drive places, we pray the protection of the Lord over our vehicles. I'm reminded of Ezra wanting to take a big trip across country, but there were bandits along the way. He didn't want to ask the king for bodyguards, so they asked the Lord for protection, and the Lord protected. Ezra 8:22-23:

> *"I was ashamed to ask the king for soldiers and horsemen to protect us from enemies on the road, because we had told the king, 'The gracious hand of our God is on everyone who looks to him, but his great anger is against all who forsake him.' So we fasted and petitioned our God about this, and he answered our prayer."*

There have been a few occasions when I have had a strong warning for a friend that they should not go on a trip. They listened to me, and later on realized God was definitely in that warning. There have been times when I have heeded warnings from my friends or mentors as well, and am thankful I did. God knows everything about us and wants us to succeed and go the distance successfully.

The wisdom God gives us protects us. Sometimes the wisdom God has given me caused me not to travel at all. I was in a season where I had been traveling all over the world. I was growing more and more lonely and missing my family. The enemy was getting stronger and stronger in tempting me, and it felt like he was getting close to winning. It was in that moment when I received the wisdom of the Lord to stop travelling. Even though traveling and speaking was my income, I knew it was for my protection and God would provide, which he did.

MANY DIFFERENT WAYS PROTECTION COMES

Heeding the many different ways God wants to protect us is critical in the fight against the enemy. Heeding the wisdom of God, applying the blood of the lamb, and paying attention to the angels are all for our protection. Additionally, there are times when we need to listen to friends, family or mentors who give us a warning or council. Joseph, Jesus' father, kept his family protected from the enemy by listening to the Lord in his dreams. Read more about that in Matthew 2.

However, to really heed the Lord, we need to respond to what he is warning us about. He wants us to go from glory to glory and not be defeated by the enemy. Paul wrote to the church in Thessalonica, concerned that they were being tempted and outwitted. That verse is 1 Thess. 3:5:

> *"I was afraid that in some way the tempter had tempted you and that our labors might have been in vain."*

We are called to go the distance, and God gave us every single thing we need in order to do so. He even gave us his Spirit to guide us. He is with us always. Sometimes it's about getting protection from the enemy, and other times when we are in battle, the key to victory in the battle is not about protection from the enemy. It's knowing when to fight and if we are to fight. If you want to be a winner, don't fight everybody. Fight somebody at a certain time, in a strategic way.

CHAPTER ELEVEN

A TIME TO WAR

—

Warfare can be so serious. After all, the devil is after us. Some people are always freaking out though, and I get it. I occasionally freak out too! When I begin to get clobbered in the spirit, emotionally, relationally or any other way, sometimes I can get nervous. It's not fun, and I can get very serious. I've gotten the trophy (so to speak) for being the most intense. But I am a warrior, and we fight battles and take names, right? You know what I mean. But in reality, I get worn down by continually having resistance come at me.

Warfare can be resistance training. It's called *perseverance* in Scripture. But when I am being resisted and have to persevere, my muscles are actually growing to handle the victory on the other side of the resistance. The warfare is always for a reason. There is something we are fighting for in warfare. If you are always just under warfare, then you are missing the point. The point of warfare is reward. Why am I going through a bunch of backlash and internal suffering in my thoughts and all of that if I don't expect to advance in God?

I don't know about you, but David understood this. There was a giant named Goliath who taunted the people of God. It wasn't the bondage of the people that got David in the fight though, it was the reward. When he heard the reward promised to whoever could take out Goliath (the devil), he said yes to getting in the fight. See what it says here in 1 Samuel 17:25-26:

> "'The king will give great wealth to the man who kills him. He will also give him his daughter in marriage and will exempt his family from taxes in Israel.' David asked the men standing near him, 'What will be done for the man who kills this Philistine and removes this disgrace from Israel?'"

Of course, he did care about the people too. It's funny though... sometimes people get too spiritual and say spiritual things that sound good, but aren't real, like, "Oh, it's all about Jesus," or "I just care about the people." Now, of course it's about Jesus and caring about the people. Don't misunderstand me, but don't get falsely spiritual.

WHY ARE YOU IN BATTLE?

Why, exactly, are you in battle? Why would you want to fight for your church, your city, your region, your family, or your nation? There has to be some motivation in it that advances you. There is nothing wrong with that as well. Some people get all bound down by someone who is money motivated. David was. Some people get all religious about someone who is position motivated. David was. Some people get all upset when someone wants to be important. David wanted that. He was going to marry the king's daughter, get his taxes for his family completely taken away and he was going to be able to become a powerful commander and eventually the king.

Look also at Joab – David's commander. There was a city that needed to be taken: the city of Jerusalem. Supposedly it was impossible to take that city. David threw out a reward opportunity. Anyone who leads the charge up the mountain will become commander and chief. Joab did. He won the victory and become the commander. It's in 1 Chronicles 11:6:

> "David had said, 'Whoever leads the attack on the Jebusites will
> become commander-in-chief.' Joab son of Zeruiah went up first,
> and so he received the command."

Of course, he later died in shame because he did a few things that didn't represent the heart of David well. But guys who are motivated for position sometimes have bad motives. But consider this: often times they are willing to go into battle when others won't. Warriors want the hope of reward, and that is okay.

Are you enjoying getting pounded by the devil just to be pounded? Why are you getting pounded? Are you under attack mentally and emotionally (or however else) just for fun? Do you like being in battles that you are going to lose? I don't. I don't even like to watch my favorite football team when they are in a five-year slump. Go 49ers...woot woot! But I digress...

YOU ARE MEANT FOR BATTLE

You see, I like being around winners. I want to win. I'm meant for battle. You are too. Every person was designed to take territory. It was our original mandate: rule and subdue the earth. That's war. Someone is in the territory where you are going to rule, by the way. If you need to rule and subdue something, it is going to require strength.

God gave the Israelites the land of Canaan. Why didn't he give them some land that had nobody living in it? Because the battle to get the land was going to teach them some things. In Judges 2:21-22, God left some enemies for Israel to conquer to teach them war.

> "I will no longer drive out before them any of the nations Joshua
> left when he died. I will use them to test Israel and see whether they

will keep the way of the Lord and walk in it as their ancestors did."

In war we learn a lot. When we don't have any land to take though, we slack off, and often times those times are costly.

David was supposed to be going to war. 2 Samuel 11:1-2 says,

> *"In the spring, at the time when kings go off to war, David sent Joab out with the king's men and the whole Israelite army. One evening David got up from his bed and walked around on the roof of the palace. From the roof he saw a woman bathing."*

When kings went to war, David was resting at home, looking over his kingdom. Then he saw a beautiful woman, Bathsheba. When you are not out fighting the battles that kings are supposed to fight, you may find yourself in the wrong battle; the battle with your eyes or your mind. David lost that battle because he wasn't in the real battle he was supposed to be in. When you are not fighting from and for your purpose, you can be susceptible to a lot of warfare around temptation, bitterness, hopelessness or discouragement.

Proverbs 29:18 says in the KJV, "Where there is no vision, the people perish." The NIV translation concludes with, "...cast off restraint." When you don't know where you are going, you will go where you shouldn't go. Learning what fight you are to be fighting is strategic to you overcoming temptation and the snares of the enemy.

PURPOSE BRINGS PROTECTION

I have to be very clear about my life's purpose and stay focused on that. Why? Because I'm a warrior. I can war anywhere, but if I am warring everywhere, then I am not going to be warring in the place I was designed to win. I could be fighting the wrong battle. Fighting the wrong battle is going to be detrimental in the long run.

Has God called you to the fight you are in? Rather, did you get irritated with something that you saw which needed to change and decided to fight that battle? Are you frustrated because you are being clobbered by the enemy? Maybe you need to dig a little deeper with God to make sure you are in the fight you should be in.

It reminds me of the time when part of Israel was told to go home and not fight their brothers. God made it clear that was not the fight they were supposed to be in. Here it is in 1 Kings 12:24:

> "This is what the Lord says: 'Do not go up to fight against your brothers, the Israelites. Go home, every one of you, for this is my doing.' So they obeyed the word of the Lord and went home again, as the Lord had ordered."

You might be wondering, "How do I know what fight I am supposed to be in? First of all, it will be connected to your call. What is your call? You have to take time with God and define that. My main call is to raise up prophets. Most fights I am supposed to be in are connected to that assignment. Now, I may get into a lot of other fights. Maybe I'm fighting through something for my kids, (family is a huge part of my call). I may have to fight something in the spirit for my finances. But if I can recognize how the battles connect to my call, then I can be victorious.

Let me go a little deeper on this thought. There are some fights that seem like the right one and have a connection to our call, but it might actually be one that will take us out. For instance, a few months ago, I put out a prophetic song over the president of our country. It was well received and super powerful. God had been giving me a word for him for a couple years, and I had recently received even more specific strategy for him in prayer. When I released that word, there was a lot of life. Surprisingly, I didn't get backlash from people. It was a good part of my calling. Part of my calling is to be a prophet in order to demonstrate to the prophets I am raising up how to be a prophet. So that word for the president fit.

After that, I got provoked and thought I needed to get a word for my state governor as well. Now, I've prayed for him for a while as well, but haven't felt the same mandate or favor to pray for him. I pressed in anyways. I got a word and released another prophetic song – this time over the governor. Then, a person in his network heard the prophetic song and said they could potentially get that word to him directly. They asked me if I thought they should do that. I said yes, although I'm not currently sure if it got to him or not. But in that moment, I felt unprepared. What if for some reason I am invited to speak to the governor because of the word I released in song for him?

A PAINFUL LESSON

So, I started praying. Next, I did a prophetic act in a location where he served. When I did that act, I got hit by vertigo. I never have ever experienced vertigo before. The moment I started praying at the location where the governor was, a demon showed up. I felt pain in my head. The next day, I was dizzy, my ears closed up and I started having vertigo. Sure, it is a condition that could happen for other reasons, but I knew this was directly connected to my prayers for the governor.

I continued to pray daily with more fervency. Then, I was walking down the beach on a couple-day getaway and my foot suddenly felt broken for no reason. Now, I don't have these kinds of conditions normally. I'm mainly healthy. But all of a sudden, I couldn't do anything with my foot. I had to get a wheelchair to get around it was so bad. It was like my foot was broken. Later on in the week, I went to the chiropractor and he actually fixed it through an adjustment.

Was that a coincidence or connected? Things kept dialing up in other areas as well, so much so that finally my wife and Dan McCollam, a friend and mentor, told me they felt I was currently out of my jurisdiction in the spirit. They believed my mandate wasn't the governor in the way I was going after things with him. I listened of course, and the symptoms of the vertigo and the warfare surrounding that season lifted.

You see, I needed to use wisdom. Yes, I am called to my state of California and am super passionate about getting the state back for Jesus. It is one of my mandates and a battle I am called to fight. God has made that clear. It also fits into my mandate to train prophets and be a prophet. But the way I was going about it was not right, and maybe it wasn't the right timing. I am to be in government as a prophet, but how and when I go about that is key.

We can be defeated by the enemy because we miss some of the intricate details of the battle strategies. We need God's wisdom. I have since had a high-level prophet connect with me around going to the governor, but that I needed to learn the timing around it. I may still be going to do something there, but there is a more sustainable time and place for it.

I'm not suggesting that if you step out for God to take territory, you won't experience any resistance or even have some retaliation. I think we just have to realize sometimes when the enemy is pressing in on us it's because we are in the wrong fight or we are in the right fight the wrong way. It's commendable to be a warrior. It's even better to win wars. Some resistance is normal; some is because we've missed something strategic. God gives us the wisdom to know which is which.

PICK YOUR BATTLES WISELY

I've had to learn to wisely pick my battles. There are a lot of fights I could get in. I could get into the fight of my local church and all that it needs to advance into its full destiny. There have been seasons in the past where I have been assigned to do that. Other times, I could get involved in the church's battle, but it is not my assignment right then. It is something I could help with, but doing so would take me off my current assignment. Yes, I am called to be in the local church, but how much I am to be involved in the internal conflicts, the spiritual warfare surrounding the church and the challenges of church relationships...that's another thing.

Do you see the difference? Just make sure the fight you are in is the one you are to be fighting now. Just because you are skilled and could actually fight in a battle and win doesn't mean you should.

What has God assigned you to in this season? Who has he assigned you to partner with or work for? What has he called you to do? Think of it like being a great baseball player. Great players don't swing at every ball pitched to them. Some baseball players who are great are called sluggers. Maybe you are a slugger, slugging things out of the park when it is the right time. But should you try to hit every ball? Maybe you are good enough that you could hit every ball. But great players wait for their perfect pitch.

Sometimes you make do with whatever is thrown at you, but that is a different point. The point I am making here is some of you are warriors. I am one of those too. But should I get into every fight simply because I'm a fighter? There are times when I feel compelled to fight. I feel provoked to fight. I think fighting would be the right thing to do. But even so, I may choose, in that moment, not to fight.

Have you ever decided not to fight? Sometimes I'll go into a store and hear a parent really telling their kid off. It's just downright wrong how they're doing it. It's even borderline abusive. Maybe they're yelling at their kid or dragging their kid, kicking and screaming, while hurting them because they're holding onto their arm or hair. I'll feel the injustice rise up in me to stop it. I want parents to treat their children well. Now, there may be a time when I actually should stop a parent, but I have to decide if I really want to get into that fight.

I've had other times when all of a sudden, a small gang fight happened while I was getting gas at a gas station. One guy starts to beat up another guy, and then they are abusing the car of the guy they are beating up. There is a lot of intimidation, knives and abuse happening. Do I want to be a hero and break things up? Of course, if the guy is going to get killed, maybe I should step in. But just because there is a fight doesn't mean I have to take every bad guy on. You see my point.

In the same way, there may be times in the spirit realm that I should take on the enemy and sometimes not. There may be some fights that are an injustice, and yes, they are wrong, but no I shouldn't fight them. When you are a warrior, war is what you do. But that is not the only thing you are called to do. You can't *just* be a warrior. Sometimes you have to learn the strategies of heaven, the timings of heaven. There is a time for everything. Sometimes there is a time for war, and sometimes a time for peace. Other times, it is a time to war, but how you war is strategic. And sometimes I am even supposed to war with fun.

CHAPTER TWELVE

DEFEATING THE DEVIL THROUGH FUN

———

I can be pretty serious sometimes. Thankfully, I'm less serious than I used to be! Heather and I have been married for 22 years, and being married to my lovely wife has helped me lighten up. As I've shared before, Heather has had to tell me numerous times that she wants me to get a different identity than just "warrior." I'm thankful for spiritual fathers like Wendel McGowen who taught me that being a warrior is needed to advance the Kingdom, but sometimes a warrior must learn joy. I'm thankful for my wife teaching me how to be a husband, dad and someone a little more fun than just a sword-carrying, demon-killing machine. That last statement was for fun…LOL.

My wife and I have been in some thick battles in our years of being together. We've traveled to quite a few nations, run churches, been on church leadership teams, done many prophetic acts, prophesied over influencers, and ministered in a number of key places. We've wrestled with our own personal battles around finances, marriage, raising children, dealing with people, and other battles.

Sometimes a battle can seem to never end. Ever been in one of those? Sometimes a battle can be very serious. I've had a few of those. In the midst of the serious kind, it can be very intense. warring with thoughts relentlessly. Scripture says we are not fighting flesh and blood, but against thoughts that wrongly set themselves above Christ. Here it is in 2 Corinthians 10:4-5:

> *"The weapons we fight with are not the weapons of the world. On the contrary, they have divine power to demolish strongholds. We demolish arguments and every pretension that sets itself up against the knowledge of God, and we take captive every thought to make it obedient to Christ."*

Have you ever had times when the bad thoughts just won't leave you alone? I have learned that if I stay in the fight long enough, I can wear the enemy out and eventually win the fight. But I don't want to just hang on for dear life and always be worn down.

My wife and I learned a strategy years ago for what to do when warfare gets intense and won't let up. We had times when it was so bad that it caused great tension in our home or in certain relationships. In those moments, Heather and I intentionally decided to disengage the warfare by simply ignoring it. How can you ignore something that just keeps coming at you? You have to learn how. Ignoring warfare intentionally takes practice.

Sometimes this plays out in small ways, and other times in big ways. On a smaller scale, maybe I just finished a weekend ministry trip somewhere and the ministry was intense. My mind is racing when I am done. I am wound up! I am having a hard time even sleeping because so much got stirred up.

UNDERSTANDING THE ANOINTING

When you minister in the anointing, it is like adrenaline. It takes you high up, and then you can crash really hard if you don't know how to manage it. Sometimes when I am trying to sleep, and I can't get my mind to shut down from the intensity of the spiritual climate, I have to watch one of my favorite shows. Now, let me preface that though. When I am in an intense situation or frame of mind, I can't watch an intense, suspenseful show. Something a little lighter and more humorous is best. Whatever it is, I need a calm distraction to cause my brain to start going a different direction, rather than mulling over everything that happened during the intensity of the weekend.

Times like this are a light battle. It's a good fight. There is important strategy in unwinding and disengaging from these kinds of battles. Sometimes I need to process for a few hours with my wife. If it is too much for her and she wants to disengage the fight, I might actually need to find a guy friend or a mentor to process things through with. There are times when I'm home with my kids, but I'm still wound up. In those moments, I may need to vent to somebody soon. It wouldn't be good to do it with my kids, but I can still be fruitful while being at home. I'll choose instead to cut through the intensity brewing inside by engaging my children in a basketball game, ping-pong, a game or a movie. Those activities are totally disconnected from what just went on spiritually, but it is exactly the antidote needed.

There are other times when I am in the throes of a spiritual battle, and it just won't let up. It doesn't matter if I am at home or out and about, it is still there. It hits my mind, tries to steal my sleep, etc. In this case, Heather and I have both learned to just disengage the battle by having fun. Sometimes it seems like the very thing you shouldn't do. Maybe there is an intense situation that needs to be handled quickly. But in that moment, consider that the best thing you can do is go find something to laugh about. Sometimes we just have to drive out of the county if it is a location battle.

JUST TAKE A WALK

I've noticed many times if we are dealing with something at home, then something as simple as taking a walk can help disengage the battle. If it is a city thing, then I have to leave the city for a few hours. If I am going to stay in the city, I have to be able to turn off the battle looming in the air by connecting in a fun way with something or someone. Maybe I need to play golf or go to the movies. In any case, I need to be intentional and know what will actually help me unwind.

When I pastored, I noticed that when things got too intense for me, I could often times hear God better at the beach. You see, sometimes in battle you lose the ability to hear really well. That is the worst thing that can happen to us. We start making poor decisions. We are not as sensitive to the Lord's insights and strategies. We can get taken out in those moments. When you are not hearing because you are in an intense situation, it's important to go to a place where you can.

There is something about the beach. As I walk and hear the water crashing in, slowly I begin to relax. Maybe it is a beach where there are rocks to climb on and sand dollars or starfish to look at. Everything helps to disengage the battle and reorient my emotions and heart.

Recently, I went to the beach with my daughter; it was a wonderful time. It helped my heart come alive in God and caused me to enjoy a precious moment with my daughter. The intensity of the battle lessens in those moments. In the midst of intense things, it helps to do something fun with someone you love or just do something fun, period.

It seems like it's not too long after doing something completely different, that the intensity diminishes and the heavens open up again. All of a sudden, I am now hearing again. I'm back in the game and the smokescreen the enemy tried to obscure my vision with is removed. In that moment, fresh courage is restored to take me back into the fight.

That's also why vacations can be important. For so many years I stayed locked and loaded to fighting the fight of the location I was in. Running a church took all my time, and engaging the battles to see the city transform and the region breakthrough in revival kept me focused. I'd think I was doing great, until I went over to a conference or finally took the time to take a vacation. When I finally took a vacation, I would realize how dry I was... how dangerously empty I was. Sometimes, as warriors, we can just get into the mode of fighting and not recognize the enemy is slowing wearing us down, chipping away at our vitality.

UNDERSTANDING VIRTUE

Samson is a good example of this. When in battle, virtue is flowing out of you. The same goes for when you prophecy, preach, invest in people, pray, do business, etc. There is virtue flowing out. Jesus recognized when virtue flowed out of him. Remember when the lady got healed by touching him in Mark 5:30?

> "At once Jesus realized that power had gone out from him. He turned around in the crowd and asked, 'Who touched my clothes?'"

Samson would fight these big battles, then virtue would flow out of him. Even one time he nearly died, but God opened a rock up so he could get water and be revived. Judges 15:18-19:

> "Because he was very thirsty, he cried out to the Lord, 'You have given your servant this great victory. Must I now die of thirst and fall into the hands of the uncircumcised?' Then God opened up the hollow place in Lehi, and water came out of it. When Samson drank, his strength returned and he revived."

Sometimes literal, physical, tangible things like water are needed to restore what we lost in spiritual (or some sort of) battle that has engaged us physically.

Jesus was in the throes of battle in the Garden of Gethsemane, and told his disciples they needed to pray. Jesus was in such anguish that he needed to pray, and when he did, angels came and strengthened him. Peter, on the other hand, didn't pray, and because of that, was sifted.

Peter was committed to not letting Jesus be taken out by anyone, and he was committed to helping Jesus become king. Jesus helped Peter see that without the refreshing strength of prayer, Peter would lose, and for a moment he did lose a battle. But he learned his lesson and won the war, so to speak.

GETTING COMFORT FROM THE RIGHT PLACES

If you study up on the story of Samson, you'll see that he would fight, and then go be with a woman…and one who wasn't godly. Sometimes he'd be with a prostitute. Why? He needed strength. Virtue had come out of him. He needed comfort. He found it laying on Delilah's legs as she put him to sleep with her comforting caresses. He needed comfort from all that he was fighting against with the Philistines. However, he was getting comfort in the wrong way from the wrong source.

Comfort is supposed to come from the Holy Spirit. Comfort and strength are supposed to come from the right healthy people we are in covenant with and on the same Kingdom page with. Refreshing is supposed to come in a wholistic, healthy, pure way. Samson unfortunately didn't learn this lesson, and it cost him his eyes and the fullness of his leadership. Most of the time in the Bible, leaders who led a full term led for 40 years. Samson only led for 20. But God, in his goodness, redeemed the end of Samson's life.

How many leaders and people have we seen go awry in the church world, business world, political world, etc.? They started off with a legitimate battle to fight. They were indeed called to take on some giant and had the authority, the gifting and the calling. But what happened? They didn't pay attention. Pay attention, Scripture says; it's the little foxes that spoil the vine. Song of Solomon 2:15 says,

> "Catch for us the foxes, the little foxes that ruin the vineyards, our vineyards that are in bloom."

What foxes do we need to watch out for? When I am weak from giving out so much, I know my tendencies. I know where the enemy starts creeping in and what he starts doing to slowly wear me down, especially when I'm tired. Do you know your foxes?

It starts with me recognizing my emotional tank is worn down, and that I need comfort and care to fill it back up again. Sometimes I need spiritual care by spending time with the Lord. Other times, I need fun care and need to be strategic on vacations and personal retreats to refresh. I am called to go the long-haul. I am not just meant for one battle, but I am meant to fight the fight, and like Paul, keep the faith and receive the crown that is waiting. That is what I live for. I don't want to be a one-hit wonder. I don't want to be someone who stumbles before the finish line. He who began a good work in me will carry it on to completion. In order to keep the faith and fight the good fight, I have to realize I need to walk in wisdom if I am going to complete the race I am called to run and win the battle I am called to fight.

JUST TAKE A VACATION

"I can't afford to take a vacation." Have you ever thought or said that? Maybe it's a financial challenge or a time challenge. Maybe you are too busy and have too many important things to do at home or work. But is there someone who you'd actually listen to who could tell you to take a break? Would you listen? Who have you built in your life who can speak into you? If you are married, do you listen to your spouse? I do.

My wife knows me more than anybody besides the Lord. I want to listen to her. She is watching out for my wellbeing. I am so thankful for her. She has a much better gauge for having fun and doing family-oriented and friendship-developing activities. She knows how to do things that cut across my normal war mode of taking another hill, and fighting another battle.

I may not be the funniest person around, but I have learned to be a lot more enjoyable and much more balanced. I may not get the right rhythm every season, but I am paying attention to the fact that going the distance requires fun, fellowship, friends, family, and even food. The five F's to a great rhythm. My prayer is for you to pay attention to your needs as well, and learn balance in your battles; balance that allows you to not give yourself to false comforters, as Samson did, but to give yourself to healthy things that help you refresh. Sometimes the best way to get refreshed is in his presence.

CHAPTER THIRTEEN

THE BATTLE FOR YOUR OPEN HEAVENS

In warfare, the enemy will often times try to shut up the heavens over you. Of course, technically you are seated in heavenly places (Ephesians 2), but you are living here on earth. There is a battle in the second heaven over what will come from the third heaven to the first heaven… where you are right now. The second heaven is the realm that the devil and the angels live in.

I love to go into the third heaven. Revelation 1 says, "On the Lord's day I was in the spirit." That says a lot to me. It reveals that it can be the Lord's day and I *may* or *may not* be in the spirit.

To say this another way, I could be at church on Sunday, doing my time, but I didn't connect with God. I could also be at church and have an amazing encounter with God. Encountering him is key. We all know the presence of God is what allows us to stay in the battle. When I have tasted of his presence, I am ready to fight again.

Years ago, I was in the throes of battle…for a while. I was battle weary and didn't know any other way. During my weariness, I went to a conference at a great revival center. Although I attended the entire conference, I was still under the warfare internally from the last season. In other words, the warfare was still there, but I was attending a Kingdom conference. I should be getting refreshed, right?

There was a time at the end where some of the famous revival speakers were going to lay hands on everyone. I went by several famous speakers who laid their hands on me, but nothing changed. Then, there was one speaker. He wasn't as well-known, but he was known by God. He prayed a very short prayer over me as he grabbed my face in his hands. I saw in his eyes such passion as he prayed. He was passionate to see breakthrough happen in people's lives. In an instant, I was totally and completely revived. My spirit awakened. The internal battle was gone. I was so provoked that I went out and began to prophecy over people and pray for people to get healed, and they got healed.

What just happened? The heavens opened up over me through someone's prayers. There are a few points worth noting here. First, a great conference doesn't necessarily affect everyone in the same way or even guarantee the heavens will really open or the warfare will clear over the area or over people. Second, just because someone is a famous preacher doesn't mean they actually carry the goods to get the heavens open over your life. Third, God may want to give you a breakthrough through someone who you don't expect.

GET YOUR HEAVENS OPEN

However, you need to get your heavens open, get them open. Some people seem to carry an open heaven wherever they go. I've spent years learning how to do that. I am absolutely passionate about getting the heavens open in a meeting, in a church, with an influencer, over my house, or in a city or region. Why? Where the heavens are open, the devil can't win.

Getting that preacher to lay hands on me and getting the heavens open over my life was one thing. *Keeping* the heavens over my life was another thing. I'd be at a great conference where I could prophecy and heal the sick, then get home and I couldn't do any of that at home. It was like in one city, my spiritual gun was loaded and would fire whenever I was in that city, but when I was in my city, I had a gun, but no bullets would come out. I was learning the difference between being under someone's open heaven and learning to open up heaven over me.

If you can't get your heavens open, you won't be able to encounter God and bring encounters; you won't be able to hear to get the strategy to take out the enemy. Remember the difference between David and Saul? David learned how to inquire of the Lord and to always keep his heavens open. There was a time or two when he disobeyed, and it cost him a lot, but then he repented and got back into the favor of God. Saul, on the other hand, disobeyed and went further and further away from God...to the point where he could no longer hear God through any of the methods of the day. He resorted to witchcraft to try and hear. That's a bad day right there.

UNBLOCKING VISION

When I'm in battle, the enemy will try to block my vision. It's like flying in an airplane, and all of a sudden it's foggy. You can't see high or low. It's in those moments you have to learn how to navigate warfare. It's like a smoke bomb in a war. The bomb tries to hide the enemy's position so we can't see where he is in order to take him out.

What do we do in those situations? We have to fall back on the time-tested weapons of war that God gave us for our victory. The Word of God is always where I go if I can't hear anything. Of course, I try to read the Bible every day, but in times of battle where it's hard to hear, I begin to search through Scripture to find something that will leap off the page at me. I am looking for a sense of what God is doing, even if it is super subtle. He always gives me what it takes to win, I just have to go on the adventure of finding it. He's never setting me up to lose, but always causes me to triumph in Christ Jesus if I stay in the game and understand how to fight in those times.

I will look for life in the Bible. If I am super discouraged in the moment, I have to look for scriptures that encourage. If I am without vision, I have to look for passages that provoke me to faith and help me see the bigger picture. If I am low, I have to read passages that provoke me to praise and thanks. If I am worn down, I need to find comfort and strength in the Word.

There are different passages for each need. Primarily, I don't go to the book of Proverbs or Lamentations if I need joy. I go to the Psalms. Sometimes I end up in Psalm 100. If I need peace and a sense of God being in charge, I go to the 23rd Psalm. When I'm feeling alone, I don't go to a Psalm where David is saying, "Where art thou, God?"

You see, I'm learning in battle what weapons are needed to clear the air over my life. If I need to get strength in my core and be able to rise up and be strong, I go to the Epistles and hone in on the finished work of Jesus. I read Galatians 2:20, Colossians 1 and 2 or Philippians 3 and 4 often times. This helps me be strategic in warfare.

If I spend time with God and get nothing out of that time, then I am still just as blind when I finished as when I started. Just doing my Bible time to check it off a list won't help me win the war. I need strategic insights to overcome and courage to keep going.

Sometimes I will read my Bible, and nothing jumps out at me. It's like the Bible in that moment feels lifeless. I know it is not lifeless; the Bible is full of life. But in that moment, the nutrients needed for my soul and spirit's health are not coming to me. There can be times of feeling desperate to hear from God, and I need hope and understanding. I need to know my future is bright, what I am doing will make a difference, and this battle is going to end for my good. If that ever happens, it may be time to open my prophetic word binder. I have two of them as well as an online phone app filled with prophecies and voice recorded prophecies too.

As I begin to scroll through those, I find a sense of my future. I am strategic in those times. I don't just want to browse and partake of any random prophecy. Some of the prophecies over my life are very specific about one thing. Maybe I see one about business, but if right now I don't need a business prophecy, I keep scrolling. Maybe that particular day I need a prophecy to tell me that my family and my future is intact; we will be okay.

It's a great adventure to discover which battle weapons are needed for each moment. Do you know another weapon we can use every day? The weapon of thanksgiving and gratefulness. Scripture says give thanks in all circumstances, for this is the will of God. When I am in battle, thanks will help me no matter what. This is one of the many circumstances giving thanks will help me in. I enter into his gates with thanksgiving. The gates are the starting point of a heavenly reality.

If I can't see a thing, I begin to thank the Lord for what he is doing in my life even in this difficult situation. Get this: thanks is sight. It is the ability to see that God is still working in our midst. It helps us realize all he has done in the past, all he has blessed us with and all he is still doing now,

THE WEAPON OF THANKS

Jesus gave thanks then took five loaves and two fish and turned them into a feast for thousands. Thanks can see in the midst of a battle that God will work out all things for his good. Thanks is a weapon I have learned that keeps me from getting hopeless. Thanks helps me see that good things are happening, even in the worst of situations. Thanks helps me see what God is doing in my midst.

When I see what God is doing in my midst, then I have hope. I know I am not alone. I know God is working. Then, I begin to feel faith rise up. Faith is confidence that victory is sure. If I don't have faith, then I need to find hope. If I don't have even hope that good is coming (because the enemy has clouded my heavens), then I start thanking God. Thanks starts clearing the clouds from around my head. I start entering into his gates and his courts with praise.

Once I have found something to thank the Lord about, then I have a reason to praise. We must praise with revelation. Once we have the revelation that provokes us to praise, then God can begin to inhabit our praise. Start with simple things. I praise him, giving thanks for the food on my table, the protection of my family, and the revelation from the Word. Simply think of all the things you are thankful for and give him praise for it. He engages us when we are thankful.

Remember a few chapters ago when we talked about praise? Praise starts with thanks. Thanks is something I do often to keep my heavens open. It keeps me filled with hope. My perspective stays fixed on the right things and off of what is not happening in my life. The devil wants to get us focused on what is not happening and on the lie that he is winning. Thanks reminds us that God is working in our midst, even if it looks super small. John 6:23 says, "At the giving of thanks the bread was multiplied."

The goal is to get your heavens open. If you can get your heavens open, then the next goal is to keep your heavens open. That is the battle.

The heavens are opened with praise and prophecy, etc., and they are kept open through healthy relationships and relational dynamics. One of the relational dynamics that will actually cause you to keep your heavens open and win battles is the skill of blessing and honoring others.

CHAPTER FOURTEEN

SOMETIMES AN INDIRECT APPROACH TO WARFARE IS BETTER

———

S ometimes we want to directly assault the enemy; we want to start
rebuking devils and casting down demons. That approach may work
in some situations, but other times there may be another strategy.
When David was first assaulted by the Philistines after he had been
anointed king, his first attack was a direct, frontal assault on the enemy. But
the second time, he was instructed to not go straight up, but to circle around
and attack from the rear. See this in 2 Sam 5:23:

> "Do not go straight up, but circle around behind them and attack
> them in front of the Balsam trees."

The wisdom of God may tell us to circle around. In Rick Joyner's visionary
book called *The Final Quest*, there were a group of guys who came down
from the top of a mountain and went straight at the enemy. Unfortunately,
they didn't know they had stepped into pride and presumption, leaving

them open for defeat. If we think the best approach is *always* just jumping headfirst into battle, we can be in for a defeat. If we go head on immediately, we'll get blindsided. But if we use Holy Spirit strategy, then sometimes we are the ones who actually blindside the enemy from behind and get the victory. The key is always listening to what God's plan is.

As I've mentioned, at times I can be a little like Peter, just charging into resistance and chopping off ears. Sheer, frontal attack works some of the time, but other times, it's not wise. For example, when I am ministering and going after something God wants us to have in some sort of church setting, I may feel resistance. There is something in me that wants to take that resistance out directly. It is obviously the enemy, and I want to smash it. Does this happen to you as well?

Maybe I am in a church setting and feel a religious spirit rising up. I want the people to be free, and so I want to just knock the mindset of religion out of the place for good. *Let's just take it out, head on…*I think. Sometimes a direct approach is okay, but other times I have learned when going head on doesn't seem to be working or there is a lot of resistance, I need to switch weapons.

That is when I have learned to get on the piano and play a song. This may seem like an odd solution, but let me show you what happens when I do. That song will get past people's filters and walls, touching their hearts and simultaneously causes the enemy to leave. People begin to fall into the arms of the Father in that song, and before I know it, the meeting is encountering God at a higher level. That was wisdom. I could heckle and make fun of the religious spirit or try to smash it with Scripture verses, or use wisdom and allow people to encounter the Father and let him take the walls down.

There are also times when I am doing prophetic consulting. The goal of a consultation is to help get people breakthrough. Now, I have a gift that can see where there is a wall of resistance holding back the breakthrough.

Sometimes that wall is a person's mindset. In the same way as ministering to a congregation, I can begin to drill down on the wall of resistance. But the problem is…that person has actually put that wall up.

WHEN TO SMASH WALLS DOWN

With some people, I have been able to smash some of those walls down with a very direct approach. Other times when I feel the wall, I stop pushing against it with my words and ask a different question that takes me around the wall. That person often gets breakthrough without me having to directly assault the wall. Later on, maybe I can address that wall directly or talk with them about how to keep their walls down.

At first, I thought I was compromising when I didn't directly address the wall while speaking or consulting. It's not though, because I have learned that breakthrough, one way or another, is the goal. The goal of a meeting isn't to have a conflict, but to bring people into an encounter with God and breakthrough for the sake of their destiny. People are a lot of happier that way and there is a lot less backlash on me.

Pastoring in Willits had plenty of opportunities to take on people who were against Kingdom principles. There were two guys in town who, every day for years, waved signs on the side of the main highway in our town. These signs were all about impeaching the current president. Daily they waved those signs and made lots of noise. They were obnoxious and embarrassing.

Every day those guys caused me to get more and more irritated, and then infuriated, that our president was being dishonored in my city that way. Ever had someone you are in relationship with continually irritate you with something they say or do? A repeated, irritating habitual thing? Eventually, you say something about it, but you are usually not that kind about how you speak when you finally do. How did that work out for you?

As I got more and more irritated with these guys, I decided I should do something about it. I was willing to go have a direct confrontation with those guys, but I wasn't sure that was the best approach. But I didn't see any other way. I just wanted to get that dishonor off of our streets. Perpetuating a lack of honor for authority in my city had to stop.

Sometimes we take ownership of a church, business, neighborhood, city, or nation to the point where we want to strongly address something. It is like John the Baptist. He couldn't keep quiet about Herod marrying his brother's wife. He had to say something. Sometimes we feel the best thing to do is to be a John the Baptist or an Elijah. There actually are times where we should use that kind of approach. We shouldn't hold back out of fear.

SOMETIMES WISDOM USES
AN INDIRECT APPROACH

But I have learned that wisdom doesn't always directly approach something. If you do, you are liable to be like John the Baptist…headless. Now, if that is how you want to go out for Jesus, then that's great. There may be the right time for that approach. But at other times, there may be a better, more effective approach.

I was asking the Lord about the two disrespectful sign-waving guys, and the Lord gave me and my wife a strategy. He said, "I want you to use honor to fight the dishonor." This is a great warfare tool. Instead of always directly assaulting something, sometimes he wants us to simply walk in the opposite spirit of that thing.

We talked through how we could use honor in our city in a way that would start to beat down the dishonorable spirit hanging over our city and highway. Those two guys represented a lot more people who shared their same attitude. Some had moved to Willits to get away from the law or to hide away from authority. I saw them many times when they would come to my church with the same dishonoring and distrusting view of authority. Instead, that spirit of dishonor was directed towards me at church.

I had to learn how to create a culture of honor that would break this spirit. It is hard when you are the leader who is being dishonored. You want to complain and preach sermons about how people need to honor you. Instead, you are to be the one who honors or values people who disagree with you. You learn to value something about them specifically, and that begins to create the culture you want. Before too long, your honor of others will result in honor being poured back into you. This is a great sowing and reaping principle. What you sow you will reap.

HONOR IS A BATTLE STRATEGY

Heather and I decided the best way to show honor and walk in the opposite spirit of what was happening was to put on a special dinner for our city police officers, city government officials and fire fighters. We raised some money from our church, money we were going to sow into the city, and then we put together the nicest dinner we could put on for our city within our facilities. It was a candlelight type dinner with high-end steak and all the fixings to go with it. We didn't preach a message at them when they came, we simply gave them the gifts, thanked them for what they did for us and that was it. Our goal of honoring them was achieved.

The city officials didn't know what to think about it. Some were a little suspicious of our intentions, but we had no ulterior motive to try to get something from the city leaders. We just wanted to honor them. I was friends with one of the city leaders, and they reported to me how the different leaders really loved it and others who had missed it wanted to come the next time. It was a win and a great start in creating a culture of honor in our city.

Sometimes when dealing with the spirit and its assault on Kingdom values, we need to be more indirect. But when we are indirect, it actually is a strategy similar to David's strategy to defeat the Philistines by going behind them. It is worth it to not have a confrontation with a person or the enemy, and just because you can doesn't mean you have to. We want to defeat the enemy, but how we should, if we should, and when we should, is always key.

Some of us are a bit bold and confrontational by nature. Peter was. He eventually learned to rest in the prison between two guards, and in that rest, he was rescued. The indirect approach of peace actually crushed the enemy. In the process, it wasn't long after that when Herod got eaten by worms. That was an indirect approach that took out the principality in the area; the principality that was residing in an evil government official who wouldn't humble himself.

In another situation, I learned a hard lesson about not directly approaching the enemy. I was at my home church years ago and heard from the Lord that our church was wrestling with a spirit of bitterness. The thought dawned on me, "Do I really have authority to preach a spirit of bitterness message? I haven't been through a testing in that area." Boy, was I in for it...

Without inquiring further, I put into sermon form what I'd heard from God about the bitter spirit, and that Sunday morning preached the message on dealing with bitterness. Two weeks later, I was trying to watch my Sunday message on the church's podcast page. As I looked for that week's message, it was nowhere to be found. I asked the leadership team, and one of them shared with me that the stories I shared in that message were great, but I hadn't finished a couple of the stories. The loose ends had actually (unintentionally) made a leader or two look bad. They decided they shouldn't put the podcast out.

You guessed it...I got absolutely bitter. I got bitter for what seemed a whole year. I even wanted to leave the church. How could they not share my sermon? Isn't it funny that a message on bitterness could get me so bitter? It got me bitter because I directly assaulted the spirit of bitterness that really was there, but in doing so, that bitterness came at me and found the holes in my heart that weren't healed in that area. My own bitterness buttons were pushed.

I spent a whole year working through the bitterness, and at the end of that season, the Lord told me I was really great at turning negative stuff I saw over individuals into something positive. But when it came to sermons, if I saw something bad over a church, etc., I would directly speak to the problem and point it out. I thought that's what real prophets and preachers do, right? Nope.

He told me that when I did that, it wasn't New Covenant. In the New Covenant, you are looking for the good and not just the bad you see. If you see the bad, you find ways to speak to what you want to see grow, not just to what is wrong. Now, there is a time to point out areas people need to grow in, but it is how you do that which matters most.

FLIP IT

God is so good that he redeems all things. He gave me another opportunity to preach and told me how to preach the same message I preached before on bitterness. Same goal, different strategy. He told me that he had shown me the bitterness, but wanted me to flip it and preach on reconciliation – the answer to bitterness. You see, that is an indirect approach to dealing with the problem. It's sharing the answers and not just the problems. When you speak about bitterness, you actually cause those spirits to be stirred up.

That's a direct approach in dealing with the enemy. That is not always what God has in mind.

I've even learned this during confrontations with my children or someone who's in my realm of oversight. I can just directly have a conversation with them or can sow some love into them first, and then ask them questions about their mishaps. Usually the second approach seems to work better.

The goal is to not be confrontational with the enemy; the goal is to win. We win by using wisdom. Just like David's two battles in 2 Samuel 5 with the Philistines, sometimes the direct approach works and sometimes the indirect works. Knowing the wisdom of God will help us be victorious, and that really is the goal – victory, not just battle or confrontation.

CHAPTER FIFTEEN

LEARNING TO DODGE BULLETS

———

For a few years, *The Matrix* was my favorite movie. It felt very much like a picture of how the spiritual realm and the physical realm were. In the first *Matrix* movie, the main character, Neo, was on a journey to learn he could defy natural laws because he was also based in a superior, invisible world. What was one of the first things he started to do when he began to understand this? He started to dodge bullets. His enemies would shoot, and he learned how to step out of the way or bend and contort his body so bullets missed.

Now, in one of the first encounters he had with the enemy, he didn't perfectly dodge the bullets. He came out of the battle with a little scratch. A bullet still grazed him. If we are to be victorious in life and the battles that come our way or that we step into while taking territory, we need to learn how to dodge the bullets of the enemy.

One of the first bullets I had to learn to dodge was shame. I remember getting this revelation about how to dodge words people would say with the same technique Neo used. You have to start recognizing that spiritual bullets can be words, they are from an inferior realm and know they can fall instead of landing inside your heart to hurt you.

Sometimes, as someone's words are coming at me, and I can tell they have a stinger on them, I literally look at them and decide to not receive them into my spirit as truth for me. They may be how someone feels, but they are not allowed to touch me. Simply recognizing that they are words filled with shame, and shame doesn't belong to me, allows them to drop. In one of the scenes of the movie with Neo, he has three bullets or so come at him all at once. He is able to slow down the whole scene around him and actually pluck one of the bullets out of the air between his fingers and look at it. After he assessed it, it fell down and so did all the others. They no longer had power to hurt him.

HOW DOES SHAME FALL?

How does a shame word fall to the ground for me? By recognizing that shame has been defeated at the cross. "There is no more condemnation..." says Romans 12:1 "...for those who are in Christ Jesus." Shame, condemnation, punishment, guilt...they all can drop, and we can defeat their ability to get to our heart by recognizing these are lies from the devil and not allowed to touch us.

I've also learned about other deadly words that can be defused. They are like bombs; they need defusing. They are a time bomb set to blow up your heart, waiting to go off at the right moment. Have you ever been doing just fine? You don't feel any warfare. Everything feels great. That is, until you get an email or a letter that you start reading?

As you read it, from either a person you know or someone sending hate mail, you all of a sudden feel a bullet hit your heart. It is like a time bomb. It won't go off until you read it and engage it. Once you have read it, you say something like, "How could they say this to me? I thought they cared about me. I thought they were a Christian." Once you have engaged the bullet with disbelief, you are (in a sense) allowing that bomb to be activated. That bullet, silently flying through the air with no recognition of it coming at you, finally hits you when you name the bullet and allow its hurt to hit you.

I'm thankful for the years of having a very precise intercessor who has taken many of those bullets out of me when they've hit. Sometimes somebody would hit me with words of accusation. Sometimes the person hitting me with those words was someone I knew, a team member, or at other times a random person from online who disagreed with me. When they told me their disagreement, they threw in a couple other mean comments that accused me of being heretical, a false prophet, etc. You'd be surprised at some of the bullets that come my way from believers. Primarily, that's who's actually throwing them.

I think it's great to have an intercessor who can help us in the warfare. That has kept me alive. When I get hit with a word that is full of the enemy's poison, I can feel it in my heart. Sometimes it opens up a major attack that just takes over. It activates something in the spiritual realm around me that is violating. If I don't know how to get free of it, that word could start festering. It also creates bitterness in my heart against whoever spoke it.

I might start saying, "How could they do that?" Then, if I'm not doing well with it, I have to share what was said with someone else who can help me get free of it. I don't care how it got there or if I should have been more mature to not let it get there. Sometimes a bullet slips in nonetheless.

Technically, I know I should just be able to gallop along in victory, but that is not always the case. You can probably relate. We know we are loved and accepted, but sometimes a sneaky bullet of rejection hits us hard. It comes from someone who should accept us. But maybe they are having an unusually bad day and they say something rather judgmental or accusatory.

Normally, I could deflect rejection, but in those moments, that bullet sneaks past my armor into my heart. How? Because I have the thought in my heart, "How could they do that to me? They are supposed to be my friend or family member. They are supposed to be a mature pastor," etc. Sometimes the bullet sneaks in because I have let my spiritual armor down around that person. I have put them in the category of perfection, and they are not that.

MERCY IS A KEY

I have had to learn mercy in the battle. Mercy is a key when someone you know (who should know better) hurts you. You have put them in the category of perfection, maturity, a saint. But even the most holy saints of the earth aren't perfect. Everybody has a bad day now and then. I know that is no excuse, but when it happens, and someone takes something out on us, we have to learn how to extend mercy. One thing that has really helped me is to laugh when I recognize it. I'll laugh and say, "Oh they did make a mess with me. Ouch that hurt. They are just human, and so am I. I forgive them, Lord!" That can help many times. But sometimes the bullet still gets into the heart.

There are two sides to this coin: bullet recognition and bullet removal. If we recognize a bullet for what it is while it is still coming at us, many times we can escape it. David had to learn how to escape the spears of Saul, targeting him for death. He got good at dodging them. Sometimes I'll see someone, and in the spirit, I'll see a spear or a spear wound in them. Maybe it's a big gaping hole. Usually when I see those, I know it's a spear wound from a leader. With a little prayer, most of the time we can remove the spear and get the heart closed back up. It's amazing. When that happens, people can at times physically feel better from the invisible spear that hit them. Words are real, and words have the power of life and death on them.

There is a good scripture in Ecclesiastes 7:21-22 that says don't pay attention to every word that people say, or you may hear your servant cursing you. For you yourself know that many times you have cursed others. We have all fallen short of the glory. That is why if we are going to be a victorious warrior, we have got to learn to dodge spears, watch out for the fiery darts of the enemy and stay covered under the cloak of love.

LOVE PROTECTS

Love is patient, and when people hurt us, what protects us is love. At times, a good boundary can also protect us if someone is just going to continue to blast unhealthy words at us. There comes a time when you have to tell someone if they are going to treat you the way they are, then you will not be able to hang out with them until they can treat you better.

Elijah was a man just like us, Scripture says in James. He was powerful, but he had his moments. One strategic, fear-based word placed at the right time, when he was super vulnerable, became an arrow of hopelessness that caused him to spiral all the way down to wanting to kill himself.

Have you ever had someone say something to you that just totally took you out? You couldn't believe it and you took the knockout blow. You got hopeless and said, "Well, if that is what they think about me, then I guess I'm as good as done." If so, realize something vital Jesus did. "Jesus would not entrust himself to man because he knew what was in a man" (John 2:24).

This is not a depressing assessment of the terrible nature of mankind, but it is a useful piece of wisdom for when the enemy attacks through humanity. In that moment, we need to recognize that even our loved ones can say stuff that really hurts us. Sometimes those are the ones who do the most damage if we haven't learned that we can't trust people to be perfect towards us. We can grow to have really healthy, great relationships around us, but we have to recognize that even within healthy relationships some mistakes are made.

I make mistakes, that's why there is forgiveness. Scripture says if your brother sins against you, forgive him 70 times 7 times (Matthew 18:22). In other words, expect that there will be a few word curses directed at you intentionally and unintentionally. Forgive people when they shoot a word arrow at you. Ask people's forgiveness when you do the same. With sincerity and true humility, repent when you have put an arrow in someone's heart. Communicate to them that this was not right for you to do and you are completely sorry. Relationships aren't about perfection, they are about mercy, forgiveness, kindness, care, and at times reconciliation.

Of course, there is another level we deal with when it comes to words. If the same type of word continually gets under our armor and hits our heart, we must do something different. For a long time, I would get hit by the same kind of word arrow again and again. It was a real and inappropriate thing that hit me, but I could either keep getting an intercessor to pull the bullets out or I could learn why that particular kind of bullet kept getting past my armor.

ASK AN INTERCESSOR

Sometimes it takes someone else to help us figure out why we keep getting hurt. I've needed to ask one of my intercessors to help me identify what that bullet is, and then start to think back through all the times a bullet of that nature has hit my heart and caused me so much grief. Then, I have to break down exactly what that bullet is. We need to name the enemy's assault weapons. If it is rejection, then the next time that kind of word comes my way, I can start to recognize it while it is still flying through the air towards me. That is when my new, Neo bullet-dodging skills come into play, and I can avoid it.

Wouldn't it be nice if those bullets just stopped coming all together? One thing that can help reduce those kinds of bullets from flying at you from people you care about is having a conversation. Now, I can't confront everyone who says something hurtful to me, but I can have conversations with people I care about.

The more I have put myself out there on social media, the more comments I get flooding back in. Certain topics seem to draw lots of negative, critical comments. I have learned that replying to the spiteful comments is not helpful. Anymore, for the most part, I have learned to not even allow those words to become darts that hit my heart. I don't give them weight in my life. Delete the comment, block the user and move on is my solution. Is it my job to help everyone on Facebook and change their mindsets? I don't need to worry about trying to help everybody. Thinking I can turn every enemy into a believer of what I am called to do would be silly. But if a friend hurts me, then I should have a conversation.

Scripture says in Matthew 5:23-24 that if you are worshiping and you remember that someone has something against you, go to him and make things right, then come offer your gift on the altar. I've had to learn to do that. I remember a conversation I was having with someone who worked for me, and they took a verbal swipe at me. Now, sometimes I'm a little slow. During conversations, I don't always quickly recognize if a word has something poisonous on it.

As soon as I recognized the swipe, I remembered the passage about forgiving 70 times 7. So I called them as soon as I recognized they had hurt me, intentionally or unintentionally…it doesn't matter. I asked them about their comment and said, "Ouch that hurt. You okay? Did I hurt you? Why was that comment spoken?" They then told me what was really going on. It mostly didn't have anything to do with me in that case, and may have just been something they were going through. I then forgive them, and then the pain of that word's sting was gone.

There is so much in this conversation about learning to dodge bullets, but if we are going to go the distance and be victorious as New Covenant warriors, we have to learn how to understand the dynamics of people's words and our own words. There is such power in words. Words bring life and death. Let our words only bring life. Let's also find out who we can do life with.

CHAPTER SIXTEEN

BATTLE BUDDIES

—

Hopefully now you understand warfare is real. Some people like to say it isn't. Some people are like Job's friends. When Job was going through battle, his friends said all sorts of things that God didn't like. God rebuked them in the end and said they hadn't spoken rightly. It's not fun to be in intense situations and feel condemned when you share with people what you are going through. When you are in a fight, you have to learn who you can talk to about the fight. You have to learn who understands what you are going through and doesn't think you're crazy. I've been around some intense situations in the spirit myself and have seen some other people who have been there too. It's real, folks. We all need a battle buddy.

When you are in those situations, you need someone who knows about battle and won't condemn or guilt you or give you an answer about why you shouldn't really be in battle. That's what Job's counselors did. They told him that there had to be a reason that he was in the mess he was in. "Job, you brought this on yourself..."

I'm so thankful I have some battle buddies I can count on. One of my battle fathers is Wendell McGowan. I don't know how many fights I've been in all over the world, but sometimes I need someone like Wendell to give me some perspective on the fight I am in. He is always able to help me make sense of what is trying to overwhelm or take me out.

I may come into a nation and feel as if I am going to burst. I can feel the enemy and feel the battle. My emotions may be out of whack, and I don't know which way is up and which way is down. Sometimes when you are in battle, you are unsure of what to do and it can feel paralyzing. Outside perspective is exactly what you need in those moments. If you are going to make it, you've got to be able to trust someone outside of yourself.

TAKE TIME TO BUILD CONNECTION

If you haven't taken the time to build trusting relationships with mentors or friends and peers before a battle, then when a battle comes, you won't be able to trust their council. You'll go into suspicion and protection, and the enemy will quickly take you out.

Learning who you can trust with your battle is key. Learning who has grace for your intensity, venting and frustrations is key. I learned early on that some people couldn't handle my intensity when I was venting. They had no grid for a pastor being real and vulnerable and messy at times. They would either judge me or they would take on my offense. I didn't need either. I needed someone who could properly hear me and be a listening ear or a voice of council depending on which was appropriate. I needed someone who wouldn't jump to correct me immediately when I was not thinking right or even acting right. What I really needed was a person who could help me see the correct way to go, but in a way that didn't rebuke me or make me feel ashamed.

When you are in battle, you already feel bad enough. Battle is stressful. Others around you may be doing great and you are not. They may be going to the same church as you and even be operating in a similar grace as you, but you are in a completely different situation. They may smugly share how easy it is to avoid the kind of battle you are in and how victorious they are in those kinds of situations. Condescending advice is not what you need in those times. That just sends you home condemned. You need someone who is going to love you, accept you, help you feel safe, and then give you perspective to help you hold on or break through.

In the past when I have been in certain situations, people with all good intentions have given me pat, religious answers. One-size-fits-all answers. I've learned that one size doesn't fit all. When someone comes to me about a difficult warfare situation they are going through, it's my job first of all to be a safe place. Second, it's my job to be a listening ear. Third, and only if invited, it's my job to be a voice of council.

I was just recently talking with someone who was absolutely devastated in a situation. I could tell I didn't have any wisdom for them. I wish I did. It would have been wonderful to have had great advice to help them with direction, but I had none. I had nothing solid that would help them. This happens more often than we'd like. When it does, we can just try to help a person get clear for themselves. If they can't get clear and there doesn't seem to be any clarity, then we can just be a safe place for them during the middle of their fight.

Sometimes even the wisdom of counselors in the midst of a battle won't be the wisdom that gets us *out* of the fight, but their wisdom can help us fight well. Of course, it's great when you can get wisdom that helps you get out of a fight, or even out of a repeated, unpleasant situation.

GOD IDEA OR GOOD IDEA?

For a long time as I traveled, most of the nights in hotels or even in people's houses proved to be challenging for me. I ended up picking up stuff, spiritually, when I'd go into houses or hotels. Good rest eluded me, tossing and turning most of the night. For years it was that way, until I just learned to relax in the midst of it, knowing that eventually I would be home again and could rest. That's an okay place to be, but not where anybody wants to stay.

I stayed in that place for years. People gave me all sorts of advice. "Anoint the doors of where you are staying." "Put worship music on when you go places, and that'll fix it." "Get intercessors to go into the places you stay and pray over them." All of their advice was good and well, but it just didn't work for me. I tried it all. Sometimes people's victories given to you with a sense of accomplishment can actually make you feel even worse than before you asked for help. You just feel bad because *you are not as spiritual as them*. You see, you need people who don't try to fix you, but just are there for you.

Of course, I want to help and counsel people just like the next guy. I see people going through battle, and I want to help them out. Maybe they are being falsely accused at their church, they are being cheated on by someone or they are getting clobbered by the devil every night in their sleep. Instead of assuming I know the answer they need, I have learned to try to first just empathize with them. Even if I don't understand or haven't gone through what they have, I don't want to assume that they are in the wrong.

Job's friends emphatically decreed that Job was in the wrong. There had to be something wrong with him. He must have been guilty of some sin. Of course, if we scoured through the book of Job, we could find a few fears there and a few potential open doors to the demonic realm. Hindsight is 20/20 people say, which means it's much easier looking back at a situation than if you are in the situation currently and caught in the middle of the drama of it.

I remember an intense situation when I pastored. Actually, I was intense. I was fighting for relationship breakthrough. I was fighting to not be controlling, and yet not to be taken advantage of. I was fighting to build a team and to go after revival. It was an intense 11 years.

One time, a lady who was a part of our team got up during a worship set and started talking about the need to really worship. She used the illustration of someone who had almost gotten run over by a truck, but then someone else had helped them at the last minute not to get run over. She said it was like Jesus and how he rescued us when we should have paid for our own sins. He saved us from death. Now, it was actually not a bad illustration to prove the point she was making, but for some reason it just hit me wrong at the time.

LEARNING HOW TO RESPOND CORRECTLY

When you are in the middle of battle, it's easy to react wrongly at times when you are suspicious of people and learning to trust. I was in that season, and so I called her in the next day. With my wife there, I gave her a little conversation about how I disagreed with the use of that illustration during worship as a means to provoke people to worship. Frankly, I don't remember how the conversation ended.

What I do remember, is a few years later, looking back at that situation and saying how silly it was of me to need to make a big deal about it. It seemed so absolutely useless and ridiculous to even bring up the conversation. But in the heat of the battle, everything can seem so big. When you look back, you realize you weren't seeing clearly.

When I've been in those long-term battles and people begin to seem like enemies to me, I have to methodically, rationally remind myself that most people aren't out to get me. I also need some mentors and friends to help me see my irrational, invalid thinking. Thankfully, when I've been bitter and wanted to leave a situation, my church, or a relationship, my wife wasn't in the same bitter emotional space as I was. In the moment of the fight, I'd love to pull her into my bitterness and get her, and many others on my side, and offended along with me. You know what I'm talking about. But I'm thankful I have people around me who won't let me do that. I'm also thankful I don't go down that road as often as I used to. I'm not saying I'm perfect, just not going to go down that road anymore. It's no fun.

All this to say that we do need the right people in our lives when we are in battles; people who get us, love us, accept us and can call us on our irrational thinking or actions when we are about ready to do something that would truly hurt us or those around us. Warfare comes and goes. If you have the right people in your corner, know how to hear God, and keep walking until you hear God, then you will make it through the fight and finish the battle victoriously.

That's my goal: to fight the fight and to win the prize at the end, and to hear the words, "Well done, good and faithful son." Of course, I do live with the well done, good and faithful now, but I know there is one coming at the end of the fight when all the battles are over.

CONCLUSIONS

Thank you for going on this journey with me to discover a little more about how to walk out your battle in a New Covenant way. I hope my vulnerability gave you hope. Being transparent and real was important to me so you wouldn't think it's only you who wrestles with certain things. You need to know that even though I'm a writer, a prophet, a third-generation pastor, a beloved son, a happily married husband, and a happy father, that I am also human. I have had to wrestle with the enemy, get beat up a few thousand times, learn how to overcome, and stay in the fight.

Here I am. I may have a few battle scars, but I'm still a victorious warrior…maybe not all the time, but more often than not. Oh, and by the way, I did finally find a victory for the long battle with the hotel rooms and people's guest bedrooms. It's strange but it works.

The solution came to me when I really needed it. A fellow prophet told me that when he goes into a hotel room, etc., he slams down an invisible staff on the ground like a staff Moses would have carried. He declares that the territory he is staying at for the night belongs to him. How could he say that, you ask? In his estimation, when we pay for a hotel room, we have actual authority and legal rights in that space for the moment because you signed a contract to stay in that room. His logic was unique, and strangely enough it worked. It worked many times.

My wife and I both humorously do this now nearly every time we come into a room we are staying in. As soon as we enter the room, we put down our luggage, we take our invisible staffs, pound them on the ground and declare the place we are staying at belongs to Jesus. Most of the time we sleep soundly after that. I'm thankful I found a battle buddy in my wife, and I'm thankful for the unique battle wisdom from a fellow prophet to help me sleep through the night.

I'm thankful there are unique solutions for every one of our battles so we can fight the good fight. I pray you would have the spirit of wisdom to know what to do for every battle that comes your way. I pray you would enjoy the fight and enjoy the people around you. I pray that you would fight to the end and get your crown because you finished well. Much grace on you and over you. May his protection be upon everything that is yours and everyone in your care. Much grace, fellow warriors!

Sincerely,

Keith Ferrante

Phil 1:6, "He who began a work in you will carry it on to completion!"

Keith Ferrante is a prophetic voice who travels internationally speaking in churches, conferences, ministry schools, and other venues. Keith carries a message of freedom for the body of Christ helping to bring revival and reformation. He is a prophetic voice that carries a breaker anointing to open up the heavens and brings timely corporate and personal prophetic words. Keith has developed many resources that offer fresh perspective on the prophetic, supernatural Kingdom-character, and spiritual gifting. Keith is passionate to see the fullness of heaven's atmosphere here on earth and brings people into divine reality through joyful glory encounters, impartation, and signs and wonders.

Keith is the founder and director of Emerging Prophets, a ministry that provides resources for highly gifted prophetic individuals. The ministry helps them discover whether or not they are a prophet, what kind of a prophet they are, and resources and lessons that help develop the much-needed character to move from the calling of prophet to the office of prophet. Keith is also a prophetic life consultant assisting highly motivated individuals and influencers achieve breakthrough in their personal and spiritual life, business, and position of influence.

EMERGING PROPHET SCHOOL

If you are interested in developing your prophetic call or discovering if you are a prophet, visit their website at *www.emergingprophets.com* to find out how you can sign up for a module on our online school or attend a regional Emerging Prophet school near you. If you are interested in personally being developed as an emerging prophet, we also offer coaching for developing prophets, as well as marketplace leaders. If you are interested in hosting an Emerging Prophet weekend intensive to introduce the concept of developing prophets in your area, please contact us. Also if you are interested in starting an Emerging Prophet School in your area, we would love to chat with you.

If you would like to host Keith Ferrante or one of the Emerging Prophet trainers to minister in your area, please contact us.

www.emergingprophets.com

MORE RESOURCES FROM KEITH FERRANTE

BOOKS:

- *The Happy Prophet*
- *Partnering with Angels*
- *New Covenant Prophet*
- *Embracing the Emerging Prophets*
- *There must be More*
- *Keys to Abundance*
- *Restoring the Fathers Heart*
- *Reforming the Church from a House to a Home*
- *Emerging Prophets Discovering your Identity Workbook*
- *Emerging Prophets Discovering your Metron Workbook*
- *Emerging Prophets Calling to Office Discovery Workbook*

MUSIC CDs

- Unveiled Mysteries
- Where you are
- New Sounds
- Falling Into You
- Songs from Heaven

These are available at our website:

www.emergingprophets.com